SCALING THE MATH ACHIEVEMENT LADDER

SCALING THE MATH ACHIEVEMENT LADDER

Teachers Leading the Way to the Top

GRADES 4–12

BERNADETTE BAYLY JACKSON, B.A.

BRENDA BAYLY BUCKLEY, PH.D.

TATE PUBLISHING

AND ENTERPRISES, LLC

Published by Tate Publishing & Enterprises, LLC
127 E. Trade Center Terrace | Mustang, Oklahoma 73064 USA
1.888.361.9473 | www.tatepublishing.com

Tate Publishing is committed to excellence in the publishing industry. The company reflects the philosophy established by the founders.

Published in the United States of America
ISBN: 978-1-62902-524-7
Education / Teaching Methods & Materials / Mathematics
15.01.15

This book is dedicated to Kristy Elizabeth and to every other Elizabeth in our lives...each of whom has been a priceless inspiration to us.

CONTENTS

Introduction

I became aware of the mathematics instructional strategy described in this book, Cumulative Reinforcement of Concepts and Skills (CRCS), during its initial introduction in the late nineties. My understanding then was that its use was intended exclusively for secondary math students. However, when I saw the remarkable results achieved at the secondary level, my interest in learning the approach increased, and I became determined to learn the process and implement it in my fourth and fifth grade classes. From the very outset, my students demonstrated such remarkable success, that my elementary colleagues have now begun to use this approach. Therefore, I was delighted when the authors asked me to write this Introduction to Climbing the Math Achievement Ladder: Teachers Leading the Way to the Top. I sincerely believe that all teachers who implement CRCS in their classes will be amazed at their students' success in math.

For the past ten years as an elementary school teacher, I have used CRCS with my fourth and fifth grade math students. I teach the "intensive" math population, a group comprised exclusively of students who have scored in the lowest 25th percentile of their grade level, based on the results of the Florida Comprehensive Assessment Test (FCAT). This population is generally made up of students who are designated as English Language Learners (ELL), or enrolled in Exceptional Student Education (ESE). Almost all have a very low Socio-Economic Status (SES). In Florida, the state establishes a standard for the expected progress of students during each given school year, designated as the Annual Yearly Progress (AYP). This standard is determined by students' status on the Developmental Scale Score (DSS). Since I began using CRCS, on average, my students have consistently exceeded Florida's AYP, an extraordinary accomplishment, considering their assessed academic limitations.

The level of success that I have seen with my students extends also to the secondary level. A middle school teacher in this district implemented CRCS in his seventh and eighth grade classes and was astounded to see the immediate improvement in his students' math skills. These students have all been staffed into Exceptional Student Education (ESE) and receive their instruction in a self-contained, intensive learning environment. Most of them have specific learning disabilities and are initially assessed as being from two to six years behind in grade level. On average, for the past five years, these students have consistently exceeded the school's overall average gains. Periodically, they have even gained more than the school district's average gains. This teacher, after having been trained in CRCS and implementing it in his classroom, is adamant that his students' gains are a result of the cumulative repetition that CRCS requires. He found the CRCS program easy to implement and claims it did not require that he change his personal teaching style. He is still able to design and implement his own lessons, but CRCS has enabled him to structure lessons to provide cumulative assessment and re-teaching, so that students receive immediate feedback and take ownership of their learning.

Although the CRCS approach has been very effective with elementary and secondary math students in Florida, some teachers in other states have seen remarkable success when implementing this approach. CRCS has also been shown to be successful, for example, with Texas high school juniors and seniors enrolled in Algebra II. Texas has not adopted the Common Core Standards and the state assessment tests are different than those required in Florida. However, when the Algebra II teacher implemented CRCS in her classroom, her students scored higher than any others in the school on the Texas statewide Criterion Based Assessment (CBA). When compared with all Algebra II classes in that school district, they scored third from the top. Also, that school district requires that every school design a Common Assessment Test for use within the school. Again, the

CRCS students scored the highest in the school, even higher than those students enrolled in Advanced Placement Algebra II.

Many teachers using CRCS cite different aspects of the approach that they believe make it work. For some, it is the repetition and immediate reinforcement that brings success; others claim that it is the cumulative learning emphasis that makes it work, while still others point to the strong structured environment and constant time on task. However, all CRCS teachers that I have encountered agree that the strongest aspect of this approach is its underlying philosophy that all students can learn - that everyone in the classroom, regardless of exceptionality, language limitations or socio-economic level, can be a successful learner and that this success will stimulate a student's self-esteem to a level of confidence that will overcome other barriers.

In Florida, the state has established the Annual Yearly Progress expectation, and teachers are held accountable to ensure that that growth occurs. With CRCS, teachers know that their students will meet AYP and beyond, and are relieved of the stress faced by other teachers. As you read the following pages, you will see many of the teaching strategies that you have used over the years. The difference here is that CRCS has pulled together the best of the best to make a total instructional approach that really works!

Darcy Armeros, teacher
Lee County, Florida

Stoking The Coals: Teachers Leading The Way

I. Establishing the Need for Change

A. Setting the Stage:

Teachers are the heart and soul of the educational process. They are the driving force that enables students to learn, the caboose that pushes the train along the track and the engine that powers it forward. Students are the focus of every drop of energy that teachers pour into their classroom experience everyday. Real learning begins when teachers and students interact directly in a positive learning environment.

Those politicians who have presumed to design solutions to the alleged failure of American public schools have done little to actually focus on the instructional process. Our children have been victimized by this lack of focus. The preoccupation in recent years with experimental efforts outside of the classroom has cheated many of our children of a legitimate free public education by misdirecting our limited financial resources to strategies that barely impact the actual learning process.

It is the goal of this book to inspire teachers to provide the leadership necessary to demonstrate that they are the professionals in education; educators, not politicians, understand the science of learning and must demonstrate what needs to be done to raise student achievement in America to a new high.

How quickly would the achievement level of American students advance if teachers took the reins and made politicians, parents and school governance boards understand that the most significant learning occurs as a result of the relationship between teachers and students? How fast could our children move ahead if funding was poured into the classroom, recognizing that direct classroom instruction is the soul of the education process? How much better would our students do if, rather than allocating dollars to efforts outside of the classroom such as charter schools, school choice, accountability, marketing principles or continuous standardized testing, we instead financed more heavily those things that enhance the classroom learning environment, such as technology, learning tools, teacher preparation and salaries?

This book is written by teachers for classroom teachers who seek to improve the learning environment of their students. It is not intended to be a scholarly summary of educational research. However, in order to improve education, there is a need to review the events that have forced a decline in achievement in America's public schools.

B. Where and Why We Started: To Guarantee Democracy

It is important to re-affirm the specific reasons why a free public education was established by our constitution. Thomas Jefferson was convinced that the new United States of America would survive only if it ensured education at all socio-economic levels. Jefferson struggled for four decades to establish a system of publicly supported elementary and secondary schools, which he saw to be so essential to the democratic process. "Such a degree of learning [should be] given to every member of the society as will enable him to read, to judge and to vote understandingly on what is passing."[1]

The U.S. Constitution left it up to the states and local communities to determine how that education would be administered, subject only to the parameter that it be provided equally to all. Only a tax-supported, public educational system would enable citizens to overcome the ignorance that could leave us so vulnerable to outside extremism, or, perhaps worse, to private control through the dictates of the wealthy. It was anticipated that the curriculum of each school district would reflect the values and goals of the community in which it was located, but at the same time contain the universal essentials to make our nation strong: reading, language arts, social studies, civic understanding and mathematical concepts, along with the principles of science, literature, art, music and health were all assumed to be part of the common core of essential knowledge.

During the first half of the twentieth century, the College Board developed a voluntary national curriculum that was acceptable to all to the extent that Americans continued to learn the important precepts essential to a democracy, as Mr. Jefferson had anticipated. This unofficial national curriculum was shaped by the College Board's highly respected college entrance examinations.[2]

During the last thirty years, however, there has been a strong tendency to narrow much of this national curriculum in order to dedicate more instructional time to the study of math and reading and to the standardized testing of these skills. Both public and private resources have been poured into a variety of proposed solutions to our alleged educational problems. Since federal dollars and private foundations are funding a lion's share of what's new in education, it appears that the American public may be losing control over the information that is provided to its children regarding citizenship, history and the principles of a democratic society. Worse, private foundations may be imposing standards, through their funding requirements, which are inconsistent with common American values.[3]

Volumes have been produced over the past few decades portending to tell teachers the things that are essential for effective student learning: parental involvement, community support, emotional security and stability, full stomachs, clear rested minds and bodies, and teacher merit pay, to name a few. More recently, teachers have been told that choice, charters and ceaseless standardized testing will enable America's students to perform well internationally on the academic stage.

For at least the last thirty years, classroom teachers have been distracted from the essential science of teaching and have had to accommodate experimental and governmental impositions on the student learning process.

C. From the Sixties to the Nineties
Distractions That Kept Us off Task

Students and teachers have been impacted by segregation, then integration, then the major expansion of private schools by those trying to escape integration, plus the brain drain created by this and the new preoccupation with School Choice. We have been confronted with new school designs, team teaching concepts and different delivery vehicles for instruction. These earlier attempts imposed on educators to improve student learning have often been undertaken without additional resources.

Many teachers have in recent years worked in schools designed around the use of the open space instructional concept, only later to see walls erected in order to close out noise and distractions. Teachers quickly learned that this concept made it very difficult to keep students on task.

We've also seen the pendulum swing from isolated classes of one teacher per thirty students, to instances of team teaching with as many as three or four teachers in the same room, teaching several different subjects to one large group of students. Unfortunately, team teaching has sometimes been abused by principals who have found it difficult to fire an incompetent teacher, and instead have "teamed" him with a competent teacher, effectively doubling the student load of the more capable teacher.

There has also been experimentation with new and different scheduling approaches, extended-day efforts and trial runs for an extended school year. However, parents have generally found scheduling variations to be too disruptive to family, home and work lives, and have defeated most efforts to impose them.

The philosophy then shifted from an emphasis on large group instruction, to smaller student community groups, then to individualized instruction, where teachers are asked to meet the individual needs of each student. Although teaching students individually may seem that it would be easier than teaching larger groups in the traditional lock-step process, the reality is that individualized approaches to effective instruction require the teacher's total, complete absorption during every minute of class time. Even with committed, energetic and enthusiastic teachers, the individualized approach is so taxing that this enthusiasm wanes quickly unless class size is significantly reduced.

Nonetheless, teachers have continued to teach and students have continued to learn while all of these distractions have occurred around them. A thoughtful combination of most of these concepts, coupled with sufficient training and resources, could make a positive impact on the student learning environment if used as intended. Most of these efforts were at least aimed at enhancing the relationship between teacher and learner in a positive way.

More recently, however, there have been several forays into the world of improving student learning outcomes that have been both very expensive and minimally effective. These experimental quick-fix approaches have given little credence to the essential teacher/student relationship required for improved learning. Many of these have caused an adverse impact on the basic structure and governance of American public school education.

D. From a Nation at Risk to a Nation on the Brink

A national evaluation of American public education, *A Nation at Risk** (ANAR), was published in 1983 by the National Commission on Excellence in Education.[4] The report generally found that there had been a decline in America's ability to compete with the public school education of other countries. A series of significant reforms were recommended:

1. stronger high school requirements

2. higher standards for academic performance and student conduct

3. more time devoted to instruction and homework

4. higher standards for entry into the teaching profession

5. better salaries for teachers

Ironically, although the report was issued during President Reagan's administration, it did not recommend the use of vouchers, which he strongly advocated. Nor was there mention in *A Nation at Risk* of charter schools, school choice, or increased standardized testing. Yet, the American public schools have since been inundated with these concepts to the extent that many traditional schools have been closed, while many remaining public schools have experienced an inordinate brain drain to charter or private voucher schools. In addition, public school teachers are now punished if their students don't excel on standardized tests. This retribution takes the form of teachers being deprived of merit pay, pensions, tenure and, in some states, the right to bargain collectively.

II. Questionable Efforts to Make Change

Diane Ravitch is a well known educator and writer, with more than forty years experience in research and education. In her book, *The Death and Life of the Great American School System: How Testing and Choice are Undermining Education,* she presents an exceptional analysis of the impact of varying governmental and private foundation efforts on education since *A Nation at Risk* was published. Ms. Ravitch points out:

> It (ANAR) did not refer to market based competition, choice among schools...restructuring schools or school systems; it said nothing about closing schools, privatization, state takeover of (school) districts, or other heavy handed forms of accountability... (rather) it addressed problems that were intrinsic to schooling, such as curriculum, graduation requirements, teacher preparation, and the quality of textbooks; it said nothing about the governance or organization of school districts.[5]

A Nation at Risk was a very straightforward and comprehensive report that focused clearly on the need to improve the curriculum, teaching strategies, teacher preparation and teacher pay. It identified the need to increase the amount of time that students spent in actual instruction, including the recommendation of a longer school day and a longer teacher work year. It did not recommend the various trial and error methods that have occurred since.

In April, 2013, there was a flurry of articles on education recognizing the 30th anniversary of the publication of the ANAR report. The Associated Press published an article by Phillip Elliott, *Three Decades Later, Is U.S. Still 'A Nation at Risk'?* quoting Reagan's Secretary of Education, William Bennett. "...we're spending twice as much money on education (today) as we did in 1983 and the results haven't changed all that much." Elliott cited three major recommendations of the report that had not yet been implemented thirty years later: extending the school year for students from 180 to 220 days, placing teachers on an eleven month contract to provide more time for learning new teaching strategies, and raising teacher salaries. The only significant recommendation to be enacted is the creation of a more rigorous curriculum.[6] Based on Bennett's observation, it appears that if, in fact, the education budget has doubled, the increase must have been spent on other non-recommended trial and error experiments, rather than on the recommendations of the ANAR report.

A. The Beginning of Trial and Error

During the late 80's and throughout the 90's there began a long period of experimenting with cures for the ailments of public school education; most attempted cures were completely unrelated to the specific ailments outlined in the ANAR report. The federal government at first stayed away from imposing higher national educational standards, since Congress is prohibited constitutionally from making laws to affect education; that authority is reserved to the states. Nonetheless, most states were floundering for strategies to improve educational outcomes, and were very willing to implement solutions advocated by national politicians, especially when those solutions carried additional federal educational funding with them.

Reagan and his successors advocated government issuance of vouchers that students could use to attend private and even religious schools. Charter (public) schools were created in most states; any organized group could apply for public funding of a new school. Often, the restrictions placed on traditional public schools were significantly relaxed for charter schools, thereby precluding a valid comparison of outcomes. Charter schools were so named because the sponsors had to create a set of rules, or charter, by which it would be governed. The charter usually had first to be reviewed and approved by local school districts. The political implications for school board members seeking approval from local organizations, were glaringly obvious. Local organizations and private groups quickly started seeking funding for their unique visions of how a school should be run, and suddenly political entities began deciding what was best for public education. Sadly, these decisions were often based on the needs of politicians rather than the needs of children.

B. Lingering Results of Trial and Error

There are now many charter schools nationally, funded by either private philanthropic foundations or by funds that have been siphoned from the existing state public school coffers. A large share of federal educational grant money has been provided to organizations willing to sponsor and support charter schools. Although the state has the sole power to govern public schools, the federal government has given vast awards in the form of grants to those states that comply with certain requirements, especially those consistent with federal educational political philosophy. For example, President Obama has recently required that states, before being allocated federal dollars from The Race to the Top budget, must agree to 1) suspend any existing state limits on the number of charter schools; and 2) use student test scores as a factor in determining to teacher pay.[7]

1. Outcomes for School Choice and Charter Schools

Although School Choice and Charter Schools continue to be very popular nationally, enough time has evolved since the inception of these movements to be able to assess their contribution to the improvement of student learning.

The general conclusion regarding charter schools and vouchers seems to suggest a toss-up: some charters have significantly advanced learning, while some have seriously adversely affected the institution of American public schooling. The most successful charters have generally been those that have personnel so dedicated that they have devoted twelve hours a day to the school week and extended to six more hours for Saturday School. Although this dedication is very commendable, it is unrealistic to expect that it be required in order to effect student success, without significant increases in teacher salaries.

Wendy Kopp, author of, *A Chance to Make History, What Works and What Doesn't Work,* founded Teach for America, an organization that recruits students out of college to teach in charter schools and public schools across America. An advocate of transformational change for students from lower socioeconomic environments, Ms. Kopp has found that student success in private, traditional public and charter schools is dependent largely on the enthusiasm and hard work of those involved, and cites Leslie Jacobs in support of that claim.

> Leslie Jacobs-the long time advocate of educational change in New Orleans-has seen the power of charter schools to transform education. But she cautions against assuming that it is the charter that drives the success. 'One hundred percent of a school's success is the quality of the leader and the teachers...'
>
> ...Vouchers produce transformational change for children and families only if there are really good schools where the vouchers can be used, and there's simply no way around the hard work of creating those schools.
>
> Despite high hopes that the market pressure created in a voucher system would improve outcomes for children by creating

competition among schools, the empirical evidence around voucher success is somewhat mixed and, where positive, suggests only incremental impact.[8]

Diane Ravitch served under President George H.W. Bush as Assistant Secretary to Lamar Alexander, in charge of the Office of Educational Research and Improvement. In *The Death and Life of the Great American School System,* Ms. Ravitch tells us that she had originally been very enthusiastic about the possibilities for education to be found in the earlier focus on testing, accountability, choice and other aspects of NCLB and the educational reform movement. However, she now finds that our country's preoccupation with such reforms has distracted us from the "steadiness of purpose" needed to improve our schools.

> When the 2007 NAEP test results were released, they showed that students in charter schools had lower scores than students in public in fourth grade reading, fourth-grade mathematics and eighth grade mathematics. Only in eighth grade reading did charter students score the same as public school students.[9]

Generally, it appears that it is the hard work of teachers and administrators, rather than the charter school or the voucher system, that makes the difference in improving student learning. Imagine the potential for improved achievement if governments provided the same support, reward and opportunity to our public school teachers, and perhaps relaxed some of the archaic restrictions by which our public schools are bound, as they have done with charter schools.

2. Outcomes for Business Theories, Tests and Accountability

The overall effectiveness of the use of charter schools and vouchers is still being debated. However, the issues of accountability, standardized testing and school level governance by non-educators, particularly as stated in the No Child Left Behind (NCLB) legislation, have incited a strong surge of angry response nationwide.

When President Bush signed the NCLB bill into law in January of 2002, it established requirements that affected every public school in America. The objective was to force gains in educational achievement through significant changes in the nation's approach to testing; the outcome is still being felt. In 2011, *Education Week* summarized the key NCLB requirements regarding testing as they had been revised to that point:

> **Annual Testing:**By the 2005-06 school year, states were required to begin testing students in grades 3-8 annually in reading and mathematics. By 2007-08, they had to test students in science at least once in elementary, middle and high school. The tests had to be aligned with state academic standards. A sample of 4th and 8th graders in each state also had to participate in the National Assessment of Educational Progress testing program in reading and math every other year to provide a point of comparison for state test results.
>
> **Academic Progress:**States were required to bring all students up to the "proficient" level on state tests by the 2013-14 school year. Individual schools had to meet state "adequate yearly progress" targets toward this goal (based on a formula spelled out in the law) for both their student populations as a whole and for certain demographic subgroups. If a school receiving federal Title I funding failed to meet the target two years in a row, it would be provided technical assistance and its students would be offered a choice of other public schools to attend. Students in schools that failed to make adequate progress three years in a row also were offered supplemental educational services, including private tutoring. For continued failures, a school would be subject to outside corrective measures, including possible governance changes.[10]

There was a considerable amount of controversy over the new law, largely because it imposed standards on states, waters that had been formerly uncharted. The primary objection was the unrealistic requirement that schools reach 100 percent proficiency by the 2013-2014 school year. As the benchmarks continued to be raised, only 71 percent of schools reached annual yearly progress (AYP) in 2006;

only 62 percent reached the standard in 2010. The success rate was predicted to sink much lower by 2011.

In the same article, U.S. Secretary of Education, Arne Duncan, explained the differences between the NCLB of 2002 and the new Blueprint for Education which changed the earlier NCLB testing requirements:

> While NCLB helped schools to focus on specific student groups, its emphasis was more on punishing than empowering. An effect of the program was that teachers and school leaders lived in fear of not measuring up on a few key tests and of being reprimanded and labeled as failures (or even being closed) if students did not score well on tests. If they were identified as "failing," they had no real choices for fixing their plan because the federal government prescribed only one track—"one size fits all." ...No Child Left Behind's focus on Adequate Yearly Progress (AYP) has put history, the arts, and other critical subjects on the back burner. Schools spend far too much time on tests and not enough on lessons that foster engagement, critical thinking, and a well-rounded education.

President Obama's Blueprint for Education may offer some relief to the testing scourge. As an alternative to standardized testing, evaluation in classes such as art may be based on projects and portfolios. To districts that seek to achieve academically, the Blueprint also offers incentives by providing a variety of grant funding sources, such as Race to the Top. Qualifying for this grant money, however, will generally still require district/state commitment to base teacher pay on student test results, and to adopt the Common Core Standards.

C. The Need for Educators to Lead the Way

It is our very strong belief that educators, not politicians, parents or publishers, have the appropriate resources and knowledge to lead the drive to take public education to its greatest heights. From the first year classroom teacher to the most scholarly and informed professional educators, our understanding of the instructional process and, especially, of the needs of children, will prevail only if we provide the strength and leadership that serious educational reform requires.

1. Concerns of Education Experts

Richard Rothstein, author of *A Nation at Risk Twenty Five Years Later,* found that the testing and accountability reforms initiated since ANAR, have been damaging to America's public schools.

> A belief in decline has led to irresponsibility in school reform. Policymakers who believed they could do no harm because American schools were already in a state of collapse, have imposed radical reforms without careful consideration of possible unintended adverse consequences...This irresponsibility reached its zenith in the bipartisan No Child Left Behind (NCLB) law of 2002... we've again narrowed the curriculum to "minimum competency," precisely the 1970s standard that A Nation at Risk denounced,... We've attempted to focus teachers' attention by a testing regime so rigid that it threatens to destroy teachers' intrinsic motivation and their ability to address the full range of student difficulties that can only be diagnosed by creative teachers.[11]

Like Rothstein, Diane Ravitch also finds that *No Child Left Behind* was a mistake, and similarly objects to the incessant cycle of standardized testing:[12]

> NCLB was a punitive law based on assumptions about how to improve schools...Its assumptions were wrong. Testing is not a substitute for curriculum and instruction. Good education cannot be achieved by a strategy of testing children, shaming teachers, and closing schools.

Ms. Ravitch also expresses grave concern that standardized testing, along with public school control through federal grants and private foundations, will be the demise of public school education.

2. Classroom Teachers: Our Great Hope

For the most part, our classroom teachers have taken the fall for the alleged decline in student standardized test scores over the last few decades. It seems very difficult for the American public to see the parallels between the decline of test scores and the continuing rise of single parent homes. Even worse, there is now a significant rise in the number of foster children and children among the homeless. Nationally, many single parents have neither the time nor the emotional stamina to provide support to their children's educational needs. This social/cultural change has sharply rent the fabric of the American family, and forged many new life styles that impact students' daily lives. Instead of recognizing the adverse influence that these factors have had on student learning, the public seems to focus on an assumption that there has been a decline in teacher effectiveness.

This is not to suggest that difficulties in appropriate parenting are the greatest cause of public school problems today. Educational achievement has also been curtailed as a result of the economic decline during the last several years. Certainly, the current political atmosphere has had an adverse impact on the learning process, as conservative and liberal entities have juggled for first place. This has often decimated educational budgets. Teachers are now often being evaluated on the basis of their students' test scores[13]. Like incensed couples fighting through the divorce process, the children are the ones who suffer most in this national controversy.

Also, teachers are being made to suffer for our nation's failure to approach education with the needs of our children foremost in their minds. In many states they are being punished for student lack of success, where teachers' blame for student failure has taken the form of eliminating both the tenure process and teachers' right to bargain.

3. Scaling the Ladder to Achievement

The ideas outlined in this book will provide the necessary impetus for our teachers to assume the leadership role needed to increase mathematics achievement. Teachers can overcome the hurdles created by recent educational experiments. Despite all of these costly attempts to improve student learning, there has been a scarcity of research and direction regarding the actual learning process. There have been few instructional strategies publicized that a teacher can incorporate into his own instructional style, and still feel secure that all aspects of the learning process have been successfully addressed. *The teaching method described in this book provides that security.*

Teachers have always known that immediate reinforcement and repetition of ideas will enhance learning. The difficulty seems to arise in finding instructional strategies that embrace this philosophy without being redundant and boring to students. The *Cumulative Reinforcement of Concepts and Skills (CRCS),* the teaching method described in the following chapters, attacks this issue head-on. Students are forced to engage their skills from the very onset of every class period. Their daily quiz begins at the sound of the bell. A total of five to ten minutes of class time is devoted to taking the quiz and discussing quiz items; this provides an immediate review of old concepts prior to discussion of new material. Before new material is presented, the teacher will have spent extensive time planning and developing the lesson, analyzing the best approach to it, based on the needs of her specific students. Most important, there is an intensive period of supervised practice following the presentation of each new math concept.

The chapters ahead outline in a very simple fashion the basic instructional strategies incorporated in this teaching model. As noted earlier, however, it will be up to teachers to embrace this approach with enthusiasm and a great deal of hard work. Doing so will go a long way toward providing students with the skills necessary to scale the math achievement ladder.

Tools For Scaling The Math Achievement Ladder

I. An Overview of CRCS

This chapter assumes that the future of public school education lies in the hands of teachers, the professional educators clearly best qualified to make the decisions necessary to put America's students at the top rung of the worldwide math achievement ladder. To accomplish this, teachers will need to make an extraordinary commitment of time, energy and enthusiasm. Hopefully, the political leadership will come to recognize that teachers are the individuals best qualified to lead this effort, and will provide the necessary support. The following teaching model, *Cumulative Reinforcement of Concepts and Skills (CRCS)*, is a significant tool in moving this effort forward. Those who will most easily recognize the value of this model will be those who truly understand *that the depth of learning is determined by the manner in which teachers communicate information to students.*

A. The Specific Objectives of CRCS

1. to enhance mathematics achievement and improve standardized testing scores for all students;

2. to provide a basic consistent format for instruction while encouraging accommodation of individual learning styles, through the integration of research-based instructional strategies;

3. to increase the depth of student understanding of mathematical concepts by improving the manner in which teachers communicate information to students;

4. to use teacher planning time effectively in order to ensure that every minute of actual class time is productive; and

5. to improve cooperation and communication among teachers, parents and students.

B. The Philosophical Basis of CRCS

CRCS springs from the basic learning theory that the cumulative reinforcement of concepts will significantly increase the likelihood of the learner's retention of those concepts. The true key to success with *CRCS* is the combination of this theory with the firm conviction:

1. that all students can learn;

2. that all students must be treated with dignity and respect;

3. that a student's positive learning experience today will stimulate his confidence and self-esteem;

4. that this newfound self-confidence will generate a mental set of successful learning tomorrow.

Thus begins a cycle of success, continuously supported by the teacher's encouragement and confidence, and driving the student toward greater academic achievement.

Given this philosophical base, that all students can learn, the teacher becomes the driving force that determines the extent to which learning occurs in the classroom. Although *CRCS* provides the framework for learning, it is entirely within the teacher's prerogative to determine the nature of the interaction with students. Specifically, up to half of each *CRCS* class period is devoted to student centered activities designed to reinforce today's new concept. It is here that teacher enthusiasm and encouragement impact the student's self-concept and confidence. While the teacher retains complete control of instruction, her personality, creativity and expertise provide strong essential leadership for student learning. In this forum, the teacher modifies the approach as needed to accommodate the specific learning style of each child. Here the very essence of instruction occurs, and the degree of student understanding is dictated by the teacher's skill and ability.

Cumulative Reinforcement of Concepts and Skills (*CRCS*) is an instructional model designed to heighten teacher effectiveness and student success in the classroom. The title is based on the fact that learning requires immediate and cumulative reinforcement of every skill taught. The first reinforcement occurs following the presentation of new material, when the teacher reviews all of the new concepts taught today by going through sample problems with the whole class. The next reinforcement is during the same class, and ensures comprehension through repetition, as the teacher works individually with students in a supervised practice at a student-paced work session. Homework questions on this new information provide independent reinforcement. The new concepts are reemphasized the following day in class when the homework is discussed and corrected.

So far this model probably seems very familiar, since it describes the format most of us learned about in our college course on teaching methods. For the most part, traditional teachers have been reasonably successful with this model, particularly if they have been very consistent and thorough with each phase. For teachers using *CRCS*, however, this is the first point of departure from the standard approach.

C. Cumulative Reinforcement as the Key to Success

Traditionally, students might not see today's newly presented information again until they approach the end of the grading period. By then, the information has been lost or, at the least, needs to be reviewed or even relearned. With *CRCS*, students will continue to see today's information reinforced throughout the grading period on the daily quiz and on the weekly test. Students will use the new concept repeatedly during the ensuing weeks. This cumulative reinforcement ensures retention.

The importance of repetition to a student's retention of concepts is almost instinctive with experienced teachers. It is reiterated here to force a careful re-thinking of what most teachers already know. Reinforcement has many positive results. The daily quiz is based on material taught prior to this week, rather than on last night's home-work, which students may not have understood. Therefore, the student is generally successful on his daily quizzes. There is no immediate negative consequence if he did not fully understand yesterday's lesson. Rather, his success on today's quiz gives him a boost in confidence that leaves him open to learning new information. The continuing repetition helps him retain the information; the taste of success motivates him to do more.

Teachers know this as B. F. Skinner's Theory of Operant Behavior. Skinner was an educational psychologist who proved that when a certain behavior is followed by a positive consequence or reward, the reward serves as a stimulus to repeat the behavior. Thus there is an increased probability of that behavior occurring in the future. The student is now motivated to succeed.

Again, when students learn a new concept, and that concept is reinforced through repetition, it is much more likely to be retained. This is particularly true when there is a positive result of the behavior, as here, with good quiz and test grades. In this case, the knowledge will be retained, the concept will avoid extinction and the student will be more confident of succeeding in future.

But, most important, all of this evolves because the teacher has a very obvious and enthusiastic belief that all students can learn. The attitude of respect toward students, and the teacher's apparent conviction that they can succeed, spurs them to believe in themselves. The importance of the teacher's attitude in the use of this model cannot be overemphasized.

CRCS was created by teachers in order that every student in every classroom would be allowed to experience success. The components of the model are different strategies that have worked over the past thirty years in classrooms of students representing a broad range of abilities. Each component has been tested repeatedly, then combined with the other components only if it has been shown to make a positive impact on the overall approach.

II. Rungs in the Ladder to Student Success

Both the philosophical basis and the mechanical components of *CRCS* come together to enable student success. All parts of this process have been carefully researched and included in this process only after lengthy use has proven that they are essential to succeeding with *CRCS*.

A. A Self-fulfilling Prophecy

Elementary teachers at all grade levels have expressed their frustration with students who have come to them unprepared to succeed at their new level. Middle school teachers complain of their students' lack of the basic skills needed for middle school curriculum. High school teachers find that students don't demonstrate knowledge of the prerequisites for the courses they teach. At all levels of education, these perceptions sometimes enable teachers to abdicate their responsibility for student learning. Some teachers insist that students can't succeed in their class because they have not been properly prepared beforehand; that someone else created this problem before they became involved.

In a 2012 research study comparing American teachers to teachers in Hong Kong, Chinese teachers reported that the cause of student failures in their math classes was a result of the teacher's need for stronger instructional skills; American teachers, however, consistently blame student failures on student lack of prior preparation.[14]

Sadly, students often perceive this. They accept that they are unable to succeed, because those around them have low expectations of them. Both students and teachers choose not to take ownership of the problems related to student lack of preparedness. Children who are at the lower ability levels, or who live in a lower socioeconomic level where parent support may be lacking, often enter the education process with a low sense of self-esteem. When the teacher demonstrates a lack of confidence in the student, failure becomes a self-fulfilling prophecy.

These observations led to the development of *CRCS*. It is clear in *CRCS* that the teacher believes that the student can and will succeed; the teacher demeanor of enthusiasm, excitement and energy confirms this. It is apparent when the teacher is receptive to *all* student questions that there is respect for the ability of each student. When every child is treated with respect, it enhances his belief in himself.

B. Five Building Blocks: The Foundation for Success

There are five building blocks which constitute the structure of the teaching model, *Cumulative Reinforcement of Concepts and Skills* (*CRCS*):

1. *CRCS* expands students' knowledge and skills by building on their prior knowledge, skills and experience. i.e., by connecting the known to the unknown, and then reinforcing this new knowledge by cumulatively testing it every day.

2. *CRCS* is an instructional approach which incorporates the different ways in which diverse students can learn. This is done through a supervised practice of each day's new concept using

a variety of strategies simultaneously, so that every student's learning style is accommodated.

3. *CRCS* is designed to teach every student in every classroom; it is based on the assumption that all students can learn. It is not designed specifically for slow learners or children of poverty; it incorporates strategies to challenge all students, including those who learn most quickly. Accordingly, *CRCS* can be used by all teachers at all levels of instruction.

4. *CRCS* enables students to demonstrate the necessary skills to formulate problems, to solve problems and to use analytical reasoning skills. These are elements essential to understanding mathematical and scientific concepts, to analyzing historical and political facts, and to identifying the structural framework of language.

5. *CRCS* enhances the students' confidence and develops students' positive disposition toward learning which evolves as a result of daily success in the classroom.

C. Pilot Studies: Proving We Can Scale the Mathematics Ladder

The effectiveness of the *CRCS* model was studied in an informal pilot program over several years, and many of the teachers who were then trained to use the *CRCS* approach continue to use it successfully. The first pilot program was held at Riverdale High School in Lee County, Florida.

1. Pre-Algebra Sample

The curriculum for Algebra I was taught to six classes of students who were enrolled in a Pre-Algebra class (the pilot group). Pre-Algebra is an alternative course generally taught to students at the seventh to ninth grade levels who have been pre-determined to lack the necessary foundation to succeed in the regular Algebra I class.

Neither the pilot students nor their parents were told that the actual curriculum for Algebra I was being taught to the Pre-Algebra classes. This was done to be certain that students and parents were not affected by pre-conceived fears of the Algebra I course.

In using the *CRCS* approach, teachers of the pilot classes constantly reinforced all previously taught skills prior to beginning new material. Quizzes on established skills were held daily. Students were tested weekly on **both** prior established skills **and** on concepts presented that week. Monitored practice of new skills was conducted daily after completion of the new lesson. As a result of this approach, many students experienced success in the classroom for the first time.

The same Algebra I district-wide final exam was administered to all Algebra I and to all Pre-Algebra (pilot) classes. **The overwhelming results showed that the Pre-Algebra (pilot) students earned the same (or a higher) percentage of passing scores on the district exam when compared to those students originally scheduled in the traditional Algebra I classroom.**

CRCS PILOT STUDY

PRE-ALGEBRA PILOT STUDENTS COMPLETING ALGEBRA I CURRICULUM	PRE-ALGEBRA PILOT STUDENTS PASSING SEMESTER I ALGEBRA I EXAM	PRE-ALGEBRA PILOT STUDENTS PASSING DISTRICT ALGEBRA I FINAL
116	99	99
13 AVERAGED 40 ABSENCES		

2. Geometry

Thirty-two of the pilot students were then scheduled together the following year for Geometry. The Geometry curriculum was presented, again, using the *CRCS* instructional method. The students who had not been scheduled for Pre-Algebra the year before, but, rather, took the standard Algebra I class, were also scheduled into Geometry classes, but with teachers who had not yet been trained in *CRCS*. Both groups were given the same Geometry curriculum.

Again, the students who had originally been scheduled into Pre-Algebra had the same level of success on the Geometry final exam as the standard Algebra I students from the prior year.

PILOT CRCS STUDENTS ENROLLED IN GEOMETRY	PILOT CRCS STUDENTS PASSING GEOMETRY 1ST SEM.	PILOT CRCS STUDENTS PASSING DISTRICT GEOMETRY FINAL
32	29	32

3. Conclusion

Significantly, therefore, students who had been originally perceived as having a math skills foundation too weak to complete Algebra I, were able to complete both Algebra I and Geometry successfully under the *CRCS* method of instruction. This was accomplished in the same two-year span as students originally scheduled for Algebra I.

Clearly this pilot lacks the sophistication of a formalized research effort. Other than what has been described above, there were no controls, no longitudinal studies, no attempts to measure the socio-economic status of the participants, nor the educational level of the teachers. Nor is there any attempt here to suggest that the use of *CRCS* is a panacea to cure all instructional ills. There was enough satisfaction on the part of school administrators, however, to allow *CRCS* teachers to share their approach with other teachers. Teacher training modules were then developed, and the instructional strategy was shared with other teachers both in that school and throughout the school district.

A teacher who implemented CRCS in 2012 in her Algebra II classroom in Texas, as well as a Florida teacher who used the approach with 4th and 5th grade math, reported that their students achieved much higher test scores overall than all other comparable classes in their schools. For a summary of their 2013-14 student results after using the CRCS approach as the exclusive teaching strategy for math, see the Introduction to this book. Several teachers recently trained in CRCS have implemented this strategy in the current 2014-15 school year, and are currently compiling their results, based on the district pre-test administered in August, and compared with student results quarterly and annually.

III. Tools for Teachers Leading the Way to the Top

The following description of *CRCS* components is intended to provide the teacher with specific tools that will help to build the *CRCS* approach to mathematics instruction and to enable teachers to provide the leadership to enhance student achievement.

A. A Typical Daily Class Period

As teachers, we tend to visualize the implementation of new teaching ideas in the context of a class period. Therefore, it may be easier to understand the *CRCS* approach by seeing the format of a typical class period before proceeding to consider the individual components of *CRCS*. Also, the typical day described below may vary in content day to day, depending on student needs, but the basic framework will remain the same each day: there will be either a quiz or a cumulative test each day, there will be homework corrected and recorded, and there will be supervised practice.

Because there are so many ongoing efforts to determine what works best in the learning process, the length of class periods may vary significantly from school to school. Traditionally, a length of fifty to sixty minutes of instructional time was fairly standard at the high school level. Now student class periods might range from forty-five minutes to upwards of two hours. Teachers should adjust the time estimates below to suit their own current schedule, and then adjust the amount of new material presented each day accordingly.

A *CRCS* Fifty Minute Class Period

Beginning of Class (7-10 min.)
* Quiz
* Check roll
* Collect and review quiz
* Review and collect homework

Lesson Presentation (15-18 min.)
* Describe today's new concept
* Review previous day's lesson
* Prepare class for new material by reviewing prior skills taught
* Present new material (using varied teaching techniques)
* Model sample problems
* Check for understanding (full class monitored practice)
* Assign appropriate homework problems

Monitored Practice (18-25 min.)
* Full class together
* Individuals

* Small group

* Cooperative team groups

Lesson Wrap-up (2-5 min.)

* Check and review practice problems

* Summarize lesson

* Reiterate homework assignment

The number of minutes actually used to accomplish each of the four stages above will vary day to day, depending on the complexity of the concept presented and the needs of the individual class. For example, students in more advanced classes may require less monitored practice time, and the teacher may present more complicated topics depending on the class' ability to grasp new material.

The following section describes the use of various tools designed for *CRCS*, all of which combine to move students forward in the learning process.

B. Steps to Scaling the Achievement Ladder

The CRCS enhances learning by focusing on the following four rungs of the achievement ladder:

1. the student folder

2. the cumulative daily quiz

3. the cumulative weekly test

4. the daily homework assignment

These four rungs combine with the lesson wrap-up to establish daily, clear communication to parents. Reviewing the student folder each night enables parents to monitor their children's daily progress in class.

While recognizing the importance of parent involvement, The *CRCS* approach *relies primarily on the established contractual understanding between teacher and student*; it holds the student responsible for his own success, and it holds the teacher to a high standard of planning, preparation and participation in student learning.

1. The Student Folder

The *CRCS* model holds students accountable for their own learning through the daily use of the folder. The folder represents the primary vehicle for communication between home and school; students must *carry it to class every day and take it home every night*. Most important, it holds the student responsible for his own learning success because part of his grade depends on him developing strong organizational skills.

The folder also enhances the development of consistent study skills. The combined folder materials serve as a major source for students when doing homework or when preparing for weekly tests and daily quizzes. Students must maintain their own folder throughout the semester and keep it current with each day's activity. The folder is collected at least once during the grading period; it must be current with all required materials, and the materials must be presented in an organized, understandable order. The folder counts as ten percent of the student's grade.

Student use of the class folder serves two purposes: it minimizes the student time lost in class, since all needed materials are quickly accessible in one folder, and it holds the students responsible for their own learning.

The construction of the folder parts and the purposes for its use are covered at length in a later chapter. Suffice to say here that the folder includes several pockets and clips for storage of important classroom materials.

2. The Cumulative Daily Quiz

A unique feature of the *CRCS* program is that the instruction and testing are done in a cumulative manner. Both the daily quiz and the weekly cumulative test contribute to this, because both are based on all material that has been covered in the semester to date. The quiz allows students to reinforce previously taught skills on a daily basis; it never includes questions based on this week's new concepts. This enables the teacher to require all students, including yesterday's absentees, to take the daily quiz, thus minimizing the chance of classroom disruption. Quiz questions are prepared on the overhead, whiteboard or computer beforehand so that the teacher can display the quiz questions to all students at one time, i.e., at the second the bell rings to begin class. This requires that the class come to attention and be prepared to start the quiz as soon as the bell rings.

The use of the daily quiz decreases the need for review prior to tests and semester exams. It also heightens students' motivation to master a skill as quickly as possible to ensure success on each quiz. Cumulative instruction facilitates the teaching of new material, especially when the current topic assumes mastery of a previous skill. Cumulative learning occurs when skills are reinforced everyday. Daily quiz results are recorded in the student folder so that parents are able to monitor student progress each evening. The overall quiz grade counts for 40% of the student's grade.

3. The Cumulative Test

Only up to twenty percent of the issues tested weekly will be based on concepts taught in the preceding four days; the remaining questions on the test are based on material learned prior to this week. This forces a continuous, cumulative review of prior learning. No completed test may be submitted to the teacher until the entire class is finished; therefore, students must come to class prepared with alternative work in the event that they finish the test early. This eliminates distractions and added stress for students who require the entire period to complete their work.

Cumulative tests are returned to students at the very beginning of the next class if at all possible. This rule is designed to provide a smooth continuum of learning prior to beginning new work.

Students are also responsible for completing a corrections sheet after each cumulative weekly test is returned. On the correction sheet, students re-address each incorrect answer from their test, demonstrating the correct response and showing how the student arrived at that response. Since many test errors are a result of carelessness rather than a lack of understanding of the concept, students become more conscious of careless errors on future tests and have increased confidence in their ability to understand new concepts. Correction sheets submitted for teacher review are recorded as bonus homework assignments.

Students are encouraged to retain weekly tests and correction sheets in their folders to facilitate review for future cumulative tests.

4. Homework and Lesson Wrap-up

Homework is assigned every night except weekends. The homework assignment is recorded in the Student Folder at the end of each day's class notes, and is therefore available for parents to check each night. There is often time provided in class for students to begin their homework. If students are able to complete their assignment during other time periods of the school day, their completed homework is placed in the Student Folder so that it is ready for class the next day. The student will be able to evidence to his parents that night that his homework is complete by showing his folder. Homework is reviewed and discussed on the day it is due, it is collected and a checkmark is placed by the student's name in the roll book. Homework makes up ten percent (10%) of the grade; the homework grade is based only on the *completion* of the homework, not on the *correctness*.

It is the fact of *completion* that is graded since that evidences that practice has occurred, not the *accuracy* of the work.

Therefore, every student who completes every homework assignment and submits it in class receives the full ten percent (10%) toward his grade. This adds to the student's confidence in being able to make a good overall grade.

5. Summary

These four tools of the class period, i.e., the folder, daily cumulative quiz, cumulative test and homework, are the pieces that establish the structure of the *CRCS* approach. They are essential to successful use of *CRCS*, since they govern classroom management and organization, and set the tone for classroom success, while holding the students responsible for their daily work. They are four critical rungs on the ladder to achievement.

However, it is the two remaining rungs of the ladder, lesson development and supervised practice, that distinguish *CRCS* from other instructional models. Both require the teacher's energy, insight and determination to succeed. The teacher is truly the heart and the driving force of student learning; in order for the student to be engaged in the learning process, the teacher must also be engaged at every step. It is the spirit and enthusiasm of the teachers as they lead the way to the top that will ensure student success.

C. Two Essential Rungs of the Ladder

Lesson development, presentation and supervised practice are the elements that set *CRCS* apart from other instructional approaches. As we've seen, the first four components define the *process* of instruction; lesson development, lesson presentation and supervised practice provide the *substance.*

1. Lesson Development; then Presentation

Lesson *presentation* is effective only to the extent that the teacher has devoted intensive planning time beforehand to lesson *development.* Lesson development is not intended to be synonymous with writing a lesson plan. Typically, a lesson *plan* denotes the topic, materials required, and the homework assignment which the teacher plans to present in class on a given day. *Lesson development* is much more involved.

The *CRCS* instructional strategy does not anticipate that the teacher will serve as a technician. Depending entirely on a textbook as the sole source of curriculum is not necessarily the best approach to the instructional process. Instead, the *CRCS* approach requires that the teacher be the innovator and insurer of student learning. Research has shown that this teacher involvement as well as the in-depth instruction that evolves from the *CRCS* intense lesson analysis, has not always occurred in the traditional instructional process.

Lesson development under *CRCS* is a much more involved process, and must be completed before the teacher can decide on the best format for presenting this new lesson to the class. The teacher asks himself several questions in analyzing the concepts in a new lesson:

a. What previous skills are required for mastery of this (new) concept, idea, skill?

b. Of the previous skills required, which do the students need to review beforehand?

c. How can the teacher relate the skill to recent class subject matter, the student's past or the real world?

d. What are the steps involved *for the student* in learning the new skill?

e. How much depth does the teacher expect from today's lesson?

f. Which problems from the textbook are appropriate to assign, based on what the teacher will cover in today's class, as well as in prior classes? Would it be better to design new problems, rather than using the textbook?

Each of these questions is considered in depth in the Lesson Development chapter.

2. Lesson Presentation

The lesson presentation is what the teacher actually presents to students in the classroom, following the quiz and homework review. It includes a series of steps ranging from describing the new concept, to conducting a discussion of its application, to solving and discussing sample related problems. The time devoted beforehand to lesson development insures a clear, precise presentation of new information.

3. Practice and Beyond

Instructional techniques must be varied to meet the needs of a broad range of students. To accomplish this, the supervised practice period is the essential element that enables students who have grasped today's concept to go beyond this lesson, and still enables other students to receive individualized assistance to ensure understanding. The use of small groups enhances cooperative learning, enabling the teacher to focus on those students who have not yet fully understood today's lesson, but at the same time allowing other students to move forward in the learning process. Supervised practice should receive as much time allowance as possible, since this is the period where students receive the most individualized instruction. We have said that the cumulative reinforcement of prior learned skills is a constant, pervasive and essential component of *CRCS*. The supervised practice period is what ensures student understanding of today's new skill, and thus must be handled by the teacher in a very thorough approach.

> "Research has shown that students who receive active instruction and supervision from their teachers achieve more than those students who spend most of their time working through curriculum materials on their own."[15]

A variety of teaching strategies is incorporated in this phase and will be described in detail in a later chapter.

IV. The CRCS Grading Scale: How the Student Makes the Grade

A. Calculating Students' Scores for the Grading Period

In the minds of most students, if their work is not graded and recorded in the grade book by the teacher, then it is not important. This assertion does not require any research to confirm its veracity. Most members of the public consider themselves to be experts on what is best for schools because they have all experienced education to some degree. Similarly, most teachers know how a student's mind works when it comes to the calculation of final grades, because they have all been there. Most teachers have been students for at least sixteen years. Many will recall that, if the class work, quiz, homework, test or reading assignment wasn't assessed or recorded, we often simply didn't do it. Accordingly, *CRCS* requires recordkeeping because otherwise students would not take their day's work seriously. They have to know that it *will count toward their grade.*

The *CRCS* grading process is designed to give the student every opportunity to succeed. Ten percent of his grade depends on his submitting every homework assignment. All students can guarantee earning that ten percent regardless of their levels of learning ability, because homework assignments are recorded with a checkmark indicating completeness, not correctness. At the same time, completing the homework assignment provides a thorough reinforcement of new skills.

Another ten percent is earned by keeping the folder current and in good order. This practice helps to develop students' sense of responsibility and enhances skills in organization. The folder also serves as a complete source of materials needed for class, and as a current view of the status of the class as it relates to required curriculum.

The daily cumulative quiz scores constitute forty percent of the final grade. This fact assures students that the daily quiz is not just an activity to jump-start the class period. The quiz reinforces skills learned from the very beginning of the course; by keeping his own record of daily quiz grades in the folder, the student is reminded daily that he's on track and capable of succeeding.

Finally, the cumulative, in-depth test average equals forty percent of the final grade. Since this test is also cumulative, the student knows he can depend on prior knowledge to help him with his test score. He knows that this week's test will not be a path to failure, even if he has not yet been able to grasp all of this week's new concepts.

B. Calculating Student Grades

The sample below shows how the grading period score is calculated:

THE *CRCS* GRADING SCALE

	Weight
Test Average:	40%
Quiz Average	40%
Homework	10%
Student Folder	10%

To Compute the Grade:

(Test average + quiz average) x 4 + homework grade + folder grade

Example:

Test Average:	93
Quiz Average:	96
Homework:	90
Folder:	85

(93 + 96) x 4 + 90 + 85 = 931 or 93.1 grade (move decimal one place to left)

C. Recordkeeping: A Thorn in the Teacher's Side

As teachers continue to learn about the *CRCS* instructional approach, it becomes increasingly apparent that it requires what may seem to be an extraordinary amount of recordkeeping on the teacher's part. Fortunately, there are new technologies appearing everyday to help with this task, such as the new Student Responder hand held device. This recordkeeping is essential to the success of the program, because every part of a student's work is computed as part of his grade.

There are several very favorable outcomes from the extensive use of recordkeeping. First, the teacher is very well prepared for parent conferences or calls because there is a clear record of the student's accomplishments to date in the teacher roll book. Also, parents have a continuous awareness of their child's status in class. At anytime, they can check their child's folder and find the record of quiz grades, copies of most recent tests, tonight's homework and today's class notes. For the student's part, he knows beforehand that he will be held responsible for any new concepts presented today, both tonight for homework, and eventually on the quiz. The student knows that the teacher is recording results, and is highly motivated to be sure that he succeeds.

It is a continuing challenge for the teacher to devise ways of capitalizing on even the smallest block of time outside of class to keep the records current. Fortunately, *CRCS* was designed with a recognition of the importance of recordkeeping, but also with an effort to design as many shortcuts as possible for the teacher.

V. Conclusion: Same Old Thing?

The attempt in this chapter has been to provide an overview of the philosophy and mechanical components of the *CRCS* process. To many experienced teachers, this may seem to be just a newer version of the Same Old Thing that we've been doing in the classroom for years. And to some extent, that is true. But a lot of those Same Old

Things worked well, and will continue to do so now, as many effective pedagogical strategies are pulled together under the umbrella of *CRCS*. Also, to the extent that modern technological advances spur students to higher achievement, the Same Old Thing must be modified to incorporate these advantages.

Hopefully, classroom teachers are determined to take the leadership role in public school education. As part of that determination, we must insist on the very best for our students and also demonstrate that we are the leaders in this profession by modeling the very best instruction. Later chapters will describe in depth each teaching strategy incorporated into the *CRCS* model. Prior to that discussion, however, it is important to examine the extent to which the *CRCS* approach will assist in the implementation of the new Common Core State Mathematics Standards (CCSMS), and other state-adopted standards considered critical to helping teachers in leading the way to the top.

Common Core Standards: Helping The Train Reach The Top

The administration of President Barack Obama has encouraged all states to adopt the Common Core Standards for all subject areas (K-12) and to begin implementing them in the classrooms by 2014. In order to determine whether *CRCS* will be an important tool to those schools implementing the new standards, it may be helpful to understand the purpose and intent of the Common Core State Standards first.[16]

I. Debating The Need for Standards

A. The Purpose and Origin of the Common Core Standards

The federal government is prohibited from imposing national education standards on the states. This is a states' rights issue, and holds that state education is the privilege and responsibility of the state government. It is anticipated that educational standards will reflect the culture and the philosophy of the people of that state.

Although this flag has always been waved vigorously by the advocates of local control, very few states have actually established clear, concise direction for standards and curriculum. This has often left district level schools on their own, frequently resulting in a weak curriculum, based only on the latest textbooks approved for mathematics.

California was the first state to infuse standards through all of the elementary grades and to require three years of American History and three years of World History. This overall framework, including specific standards and curriculum, was adopted by California in 1987, shortly after the publication of the ANAR, which advocated stronger standards for high schools.[17] In Florida, the education community prompted the state to begin identifying specific standards which would enable students to improve scores on the Florida Comprehensive Assessment Tests. Generally, however, many states have continued to depend on the state-approved textbooks to dictate classroom standards.

B. Education Standards under *Goals 2000* and *No Child Left Behind*

In the early 1990's, Diane Ravitch was given primary responsibility for developing a national curriculum in her role as Assistant Secretary of Education under Lamar Alexander. In this role, she attempted to circumvent the restriction against federal imposition of educational standards. Her office provided grants to states that were willing to establish voluntary national curriculum standards. This approach worked reasonably well even through the transition to President Clinton's administration, until a congressional storm of controversy arose alleging that the standards governing history were politically biased. Loud arguments arose about whose history or what history should govern the standards. As a result of this firestorm, unfortunately, in 1995, the Senate passed a resolution condemning the use of national curriculum standards.[18]

Although the Clinton Administration's *Goals 2000* program allowed some dollars to assist states in developing their own standards, support overall was weak, since the issues of choice, charter schools and testing now dominated the education scene. With the election of President George W. Bush, and the passage of *No Child Left Behind,* the focus of the education effort became student testing, accountability, deregulation and merit pay for teachers.

C. President Obama's Blueprint for Reform of ESEA

The attempt to establish national standards has been more successful under President Obama, whose administration authored the Blueprint for Reform of the Elementary and Secondary Education Act (ESEA). Again, the resistance to national standards was circumvented. In order to receive federal funding to assist in implementing the Blueprint for Reform, states were required to adopt the Common Core Standards. All but a few complied, jumping at the chance to secure additional funding in an economy that forced a dwindling supply of local dollars for education.[19]

II. Common Core Standards: Reaction of the Educational Community

There has been a loud response to the Common Core State Mathematics Standards (CCSMS) [(not to be confused with *Cumulative Reinforcement of Concepts and Skills (CRCS)*]. The educational community seems to swing from raves to roars in considering them.

A. Opposed

Some insist that these standards were created in a closet with no input from those affected by them or those best qualified to write them.[20] However, it has become increasingly clear that the standards for mathematics were adopted from the National Council of Teachers of Mathematics (NCTM). Marion Brady objects to the standards for fear that this approach ignores the real problem i.e., students fail because of childhood poverty, not for lack of standards. This article expresses an additional concern: that standards may create static and students may not grow academically if tied to them.[21] On the contrary, based on the broad nature of the Common Core Standards, they do not appear to standardize student thinking, but rather they seem to open their minds to the infinite number of ways that math can be applied. Traditionally we have taught the "how" of a math problem; the Common Core Standards require that we encourage students to express the "why" of the application, and to extrapolate these applications to other mathematics challenges.

B. In Favor

Others in the educational community, such as Berkeley professor Hung-Hsi Wu, say that the Common Core Math Standards could serve as the foundation for designing proper school math texts and for developing better teacher preparation programs.

Professor Wu maintains that the failure of America to adopt formal standards is the cause of the *de facto* curriculum which the textbook companies have created by default. Wu calls this *de facto* mathematics curriculum *Textbook School Mathematics or TSM*. Because there have been few standards established by the educational community, the textbook companies have filled the void by dictating what concepts should be taught at which grade level, and have effectively taken over the role of educators to define standards. According to Wu, TSM has defined our mathematics curriculum. Math teachers know that there are math topics that share a similar rationale, and that should therefore be taught together. With the TSM textbook curriculum, often this natural continuum of concepts is lost.[22]

C. Common Core Standards vs. Textbooks

The developers of the new *Common Core State Mathematics Standards (CCSMS)* recognized many of the flaws and inaccuracies of the traditional approach of textbook publishers who have until now taken the leadership role in establishing math standards by default. Therefore, many new teachers, and often even more experienced teachers, proceed on the assumption that the math textbook which they receive in pre-school embodies the appropriate mathematics curriculum for their students. In fact, this assumption is generally erroneous, but over time we have, in effect, abdicated our responsibility as educators by allowing this to happen. However, political interference in the educational process has created a vacuum where clear national/state standards are needed. Textbook publishers have merely filled that vacuum by defining the curriculum through what Professor Wu calls *Textbook School Mathematics.*

Many professional educators insist that the textbooks are often in error. To test this possibility, the National Math Advisory Panel attempted to assess the *error density*, defined as the number of *errors* in a text divided by the number of *pages* in the text, of two widely used algebra textbooks. One book had an error density of 50% and the other had 41%.[23] This would indicate that the concerns of the professional educators are valid.

This finding makes it clear that the education profession needs to take a stronger lead in defining the standards for the teaching of mathematics. Many teachers begin their teaching careers depending exclusively on the textbook assigned by their district. There is often an assumption, particularly by beginning teachers, that the textbook defines the standards that they are expected to teach.

Furthermore, since the Common Core Standards have been published, textbook companies have been making only slight revisions to their books and then proclaiming them to be aligned with CCSMS.[24] It is the important role of the teacher to be able to identify this inadequacy and to tie classroom instruction to the CCSMS standards, and not to the textbook.

This is not to condemn the publishers of math textbooks, nor is it to minimize the importance of textbooks to the education of students. It is merely an attempt to develop a greater awareness among teachers that pitfalls exist when we place total reliance on textbooks. Education experts, such as classroom teachers, not textbook publishers, should be driving the instructional process to be sure:

1. that textbooks contain accurate data necessary to teach children correct math theory; and

2. that teachers understand that their use of textbooks should be as a supplementary tool to assist them in the instructional process, rather than the primary tool that controls the instructional process.

The definition and the principles of mathematics presented to students must be determined by the teacher, not the textbook publisher. The introduction of the Common Core Standards is a very strong step in that direction, and will hopefully allow teachers to exercise more control of the instructional process.

III. Cumulative Reinforcement of Concepts and Skills: Help or Hindrance?

Given this background, an important purpose of this chapter is to explain the relationship between the new math standards and the use of *Cumulative Reinforcement of Concepts and Skills (CRCS)*, the instructional strategy that is the subject of this book. Specifically, to what extent will the use of *CRCS* in math classrooms facilitate student learning of the Common Core Standards?

A. Insuring Continuity

A key notion that the Common Core Standards seek to dispel is the belief by students that each year of learning is an isolated unit, i.e., learn it, forget it, start a new school year. There is currently very little clear continuity between one school year and the next, neither from the student's perspective nor from the perspective of most textbooks. However, a very strong premise of the Common Core Standards is to establish continuity within the framework of a given school year and to maintain continuity of concepts from one year to the next. The hope is to enable students to better understand how this year's math concepts form the basis for understanding next year's principles. This premise, maintaining continuity from year to year, makes *CRCS* a very successful approach to implementing the Common Core Standards.

One of the keys to the *CRCS* instructional strategy is the use of cumulative reinforcement. All aspects of *CRCS* are focused on helping students to gain, retain and repeat concepts learned in prior lessons. It is noteworthy that the daily *CRCS* quiz is cumulative; the questions may be based on material taught as early as the first day of school, because students are expected to retain this knowledge throughout the year. The same is true of the weekly test. Although a limited number of test questions is based on new material, students are fully aware that weekly tests are cumulative also, and will contain questions based on concepts presented several months ago. This cumulative reinforcement of concepts is one of the most effective tools in the *CRCS* approach, and is clearly consistent with the Common Core Standards' premise of the importance of continuity of concepts.

B. Commonality: Finding the Thread that Runs Through

CRCS places the same emphasis on finding commonalities in math throughout the same school year as does the Common Core

Standards. There are several basic math devices and principles that form a starting point for discussion of related concepts. This helps students to retain and understand the relationships among the concepts year to year. For example, students are taught the skill of using a number line early in their math education. Once this understanding is established, the student can use the number line throughout the year for understanding the relationships of whole numbers. Then continuing year to year, he learns different types of rational numbers: whole numbers, then fractions, then decimals, then negative integers. Regardless of the type of rational number, they can all be placed along the number line to clarify their relationship to each other. Although the operations affecting rational numbers may become increasingly complex each year, the student still retains his understanding by placing each type of number at a common starting point on the number line.

CRCS threads this commonality through several grade levels, reinforcing it at each new stage of working with rational numbers. Although these commonalities will be demonstrated in some textbooks, the use of common reference points as a teaching tool may often be lost. The importance of strategies that help students to connect what they already know to the point now being taught is immeasurable. The Common Core Standards seek to emphasize these commonalities, and *CRCS* reinforces that.

C. Year to Year Connectivity: Leaning on Last Year's Knowledge

Both the Common Core Standards and *CRCS* seek to draw on prior knowledge to form the basis or connection to new information. Students learn more quickly if they can connect the known to the unknown. This is seen in the standards related to ratio and proportion, for example, as students go from sixth to seventh grade. In the Common Core Standards for sixth grade, the teachers are asked to first focus their time on "connecting ratio and rate to whole number multiplication and division, and using concepts of ratio and rate to solve problems." In the Common Core Standards for seventh grade, instructional time is first focused on, "developing understanding of and applying proportional relationships."[25]

The *CRCS* model facilitates this connectivity from grade to grade by continuously reinforcing ratio and rate in the sixth grade, better enabling the students to draw on those concepts and skills when attempting to apply them to proportions in the seventh grade. A review of ratio and rate, and a clear discussion of the relationship between ratio and proportion will help students connect last year's *known*, ratio, to this year's *unknown*, proportion.

The year-long focus of *CRCS* to recapture prior knowledge throughout the year, serves as a kind of microcosm of the goal in the Common Core Standards of continuing to connect concepts from year to year. Teachers proficient in the use of *CRCS* will have no problem expanding this continuum of learning within a school year to the continuum of math education from year to year throughout grades K-12.

D. Common Core Rigorous Standards: Not Just How, but Why!

Speakers nationwide are trying to help educators understand how Common Core Standards are different from traditional math curriculum. They emphasize that students now must know not only *the how* of solving a problem, but also must be able to explain *why* their solution works. This has truly expanded what is expected of students, pulling them from the mechanical processing of problems, and requiring them to articulate why their process works. Because of the Common Core Standards, teachers are now required to insert rigorous standards which include high-level cognitive demands into their curriculum. Because of its emphasis on continuous reinforcement, *CRCS* helps students more quickly to master the concrete, giving teachers more time to devote to the abstract. The *CRCS* model puts skills into the student's long term memory as opposed to his short term memory.

CRCS provides a perfect forum for assisting students in getting to the *why* of their solutions to math problems, in support of the Common Core premise. In a later chapter, our discussion of *Practice and Beyond* describes how students are often divided into working groups to practice their skills after the presentation of a new concept has occurred. They are also asked to develop new concepts themselves. When students have mastered the mechanical skill, the group structure of the practice period affords them an opportunity to articulate their understanding of *why* their solution works. When a student is able to verbalize his understanding of concepts to a group of his peers, the learning cycle is complete; he now *owns* that concept; he knows the *why*.

IV. Summary: The Role of CRCS in Implementing the Common Core Standards

CRCS will play a significant role in implementing the Common Core Standards as will any effective instructional strategy. For those who embrace the structure of *CRCS* and who believe in the philosophy that forms its essence, the implementation of the Common Core Standards will be very successful. The impact and validity of the standards themselves remain to be seen over time.

Framework:
The First Four Rungs Of The Ladder

The teaching model that serves as the lynch pin of this book, *Cumulative Reinforcement of Concepts and Skills*, (*CRCS*), is made up of a variety of components, some of which address procedural issues for keeping instruction flowing smoothly throughout the class period. These we address below. The use of the Student Folder provides the organizational center for the math class, containing all of the supplies and notes necessary to be prepared for class. The Daily Quiz serves as the starting point each day, enabling the class to come to order quickly and orderly. The Cumulative Test serves not only to test understanding of new material, but also works as reinforcement of all skills learned earlier in the course. Finally, homework is assigned as an additional reinforcement of daily concepts. Together, these components work to establish the structure and framework for success with *CRCS*.

I. The Folder

A. Pulling it All Together: Construction and Use of the Student Folder

The student folder is a very critical component of the *CRCS* instructional experience. It includes everything needed to evidence the student's current status in math class. The folder pulls together the various essentials of the mathematics learning process, and provides parents a succinct daily view of each day's classroom activities.

On one of the first days of class, every student constructs and labels his own folder which includes several pockets and clips for storage of important classroom materials. This is done as a class project under the direct supervision of the classroom teacher. Students must maintain their own folders throughout the semester and keep them current with each day's activity. They must carry the folder to class every day and take it home every night.

Prepared blank half sheets used for daily quizzes, the completed homework assignment due for today, blank loose leaf sheets for class notes and to record today's homework assignments, and copies of previous tests are kept in each of two separate folder pockets.

The clips attached to the folder hold:

1. a copy of the classroom rules;

2. half sheets for recording today's quiz answers;

3. a quiz grade summary sheet which lists the student's score for every daily quiz to date; and

4. the student's notes from each daily mathematics instructional period, which also include that day's homework assignment recorded at the end of the class notes.

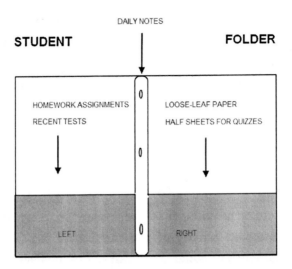

Copies of the first three items listed are found in the Appendix.

B. Advantages of Folder Use: For Instruction, Students, Parents

1. Advantages for Instruction

There is a clear rationale for the way in which each folder pocket and clip is used. The purpose of the folder is to address problems most often confronted by teachers as they attempt to provide classroom instruction. For example, in many classes, each time the teacher shifts to a new activity, there is a loss of valuable instructional time. If there is a classroom quiz, time is lost while students scurry for paper and pencil. With the folder, the blank half sheets for daily quizzes are right in the folder pocket. The blank loose leaf paper is quickly found for class notes and activities and for starting homework. There is no digging into the desk, no snapping of metal binder clips or slamming of notebooks onto the floor. The use of the folder enables all students to have their needed supplies on their desks at the outset of class. The daily hunt for last night's homework is avoided because there is a folder pocket specifically designed for that purpose.

The folder also provides an important source for the cumulative reinforcement of learned skills. The first thing a student sees as he opens his folder is the typed sheet of classroom rules. This clear list of teacher expectations is attached to the clips in the folder. The student also has a copy of several prior classroom tests in a separate pocket of the folder. These prior tests are available for in-class review of earlier concepts or for independent student practice of prior skills at home.

2. Advantages to the Student

There are many advantages to the student in using these folders. The initial classroom activity of construction of the folder helps to develop the student's organizational skills. The involvement of maintaining the folder each day helps keep the students focused on task and increases student accountability for every day's class work and assigned homework. The daily class notes, including the sample problems provided with instruction, serve as an instrument for reinforcing new skills learned each day, and serve as a reference point for students during the classroom time set aside for supervised practice. The homework assignment recorded at the end of each day's class notes gives the students the confidence of knowing that they are leaving class holding everything they need to be prepared for tomorrow's lesson.

3. Advantages for the Parent

The use of student folders also holds significant advantages for parents. The topic of parent involvement in the student learning process will be discussed at length in another section of this book. However, for purposes of this section, it is important to note that the use of student folders enables parents to check their children's math activity each night. The included class notes will reflect the homework assignment; if the student has, "finished it in school today", the folder pocket will hold the completed assignment for tomorrow.

Parents are also able to check the results of today's quiz and review the new math concepts introduced today by reading the notes from today's class.

C. Grading the Folder

The extent to which a student effectively maintains his folder constitutes ten percent (10%) of his semester grade. This grade is based primarily on the student's inclusion of all the folder entries that are required. For example, if the class notes are not current, the student folder grade would be lowered. If the quiz summary sheet is missing or if there is no available loose leaf paper, there would be a similar downgrade.

Discussion of the grade value of the student folder is conducted during the classroom activity when the folder is constructed. It is also included in all discussion regarding the compilation of semester grades. Students are advised repeatedly that folders will be collected and graded at least once during each quarter; twice per semester.

The students are always given prior notice before the teacher collects the folder for grading. When the teacher is giving this notice, the teacher and students review those items included in the folder that will be counted for the grade.

As the teacher reads off the dates of class notes that will be required, the students circle the dates in their folder. This helps the student to see which dates she is missing, and also helps the teacher during her review of the folder for grading purposes. It provides her the list of dates of required notes at a quick glance.

The student's actual folder grade is determined by:

- whether the folder contains the required notes for each date;
- whether the folder contains recent tests, half sheets for quizzes, and blank loose leaf paper in the folder pockets;
- whether the sheet of class rules is included as the first entry in the folder; and
- whether the quiz and test grade record sheet is included in the folder as the last entry.

As an example of the folder grading process:

If there are 26 dates for required notes, then the grade would be determined by points, one for each of the required notes the student has, plus 1 point for each required additional item: rules, grade record sheet, previous tests, and clean quiz/notes paper, for a possible score of 30. This student has only 22 required notes but has the four other required parts, for a total of 26 points out of a possible 30. Therefore, his folder grade will be 26/30 or 87%.

The importance of the student folder cannot be overemphasized. This description of its use may seem overly simplistic, but it is purposely presented in this manner to provide teachers new to this program as much detail as possible.

II. Climbing to the Top: The Daily Cumulative Quiz

A. Introduction

An important underlying objective of *CRCS* is to maximize student time on task. The components of this instructional approach are geared toward insuring that all allotted classroom time is focused on student learning. We've seen this in the use of the Student Folder, which significantly curtails the time spent on transitioning from one learning task to the next by making all needed materials quickly accessible. Similarly, the use of the daily cumulative quiz supports this objective by requiring that the students are ready to start work, literally, at the sound of the bell.

In the earlier section on tools, we saw an outline of the classroom procedure during a typical daily class period using the *CRCS* strategy. This outline reflected that only 7-10 minutes at the start of class is used to administer, collect and review the quiz. Actually, in classroom settings where *CRCS* is not in use, it takes 7-10 minutes just to take attendance and bring the class to order. This difficulty has always been a challenge to new teachers in developing good classroom management skills. Fredric Jones, PhD. in his book, *Tools for Teaching*, estimated that in a typical fifty minute class period, settling in to get started takes five to seven minutes after the bell rings, while a class activity transition averages about five minutes.[26] With *CRCS*, the use of the Daily Cumulative Quiz, in combination with the Student Folder, has a significant positive impact on the time that students spend on task.

B. How It Works: The Mechanics of the Quiz

When teachers use the *CRCS* approach, every student knows that he will be allowed only five minutes to complete today's quiz, and that the five minute testing time starts when the beginning bell sounds. The quiz questions are not presented to the student until the bell rings, when the teacher, either by turning on the overhead light or by clicking on the computer, projects the quiz questions on to the large screen. Since the student has several half sheets prepared in his folder with his name and period written at the top, he pulls one sheet, adds today's date, and fills in the answers to today's quiz questions. The bottom of the half sheet is used to record any calculations that the student needs to make in order to arrive at the correct quiz answer. The quiz sheets are passed forward immediately at the close of the five minute period, and the discussion of the questions starts at once. (See Appendix, Form #6)

During the five minute quiz period, the teacher marks the attendance roll, and verifies it later in the day when recording quiz results.

Quiz answers are reviewed using the Socratic method, i.e., individual students are asked to give their answers and to explain their rationale; the teacher responds to all student questions and reiterates the correct answer for each quiz item. Students record the number of correct answers, out of the usual five questions asked, on the cumulative quiz record sheet in their folder. (See Appendix, Form #4) Because answers have already been discussed in class, the actual quiz sheets are not returned to the student after teacher review and recording in her grade book. This eliminates the need for using class time to do so; students are encouraged to double check their scores with those in the teacher's gradebook later if they are unsure of their quiz result.

C. Why It Works: The Advantages

1. Administering the Quiz:

As a classroom management tool, administering the quiz has many benefits. Clearly, it is an aid in starting class on time, and is a strong motivator for students because they will not have the allotted quiz time if they're late. More important, administering the quiz motivates students to learn the skills and concepts when they're being taught, because they know that they will be tested on them repeatedly. Success on the quiz becomes increasingly important to students' self confidence as the semester progresses.

2. Reviewing and Discussing Quiz Responses:

Since the class discussion on quiz responses occurs while the quiz sheets are being passed forward, the students receive immediate feedback on answers, and thus, reinforcement of skills learned. The teacher recognizes quickly, based on quiz responses, when a concept has been misunderstood and is able to re-teach right then, while the student's mental set is at its sharpest. The re-teaching can be done through a variety of teaching techniques, modified often to accommodate the learning styles of students.

D. Material Covered by the Quiz

The daily quiz items are cumulative, based on materials presented three or more days prior to the quiz. *No items are included from the previous day's lesson.* The main instructional purpose of the quiz is to continuously reinforce skills learned earlier, not to test student knowledge of the most recent material. This distinction is important because the quiz does not hold recently excused absentees responsible for material covered in their absence. Also, students who may not have understood yesterday's concept have not yet had sufficient opportunity to have those concepts clarified. To base a daily quiz on yesterday's lesson puts students at an unfair disadvantage. Again, the primary purpose of the quiz is to provide cumulative reinforcement of earlier learned skills and concepts.

***Housekeeping Note: If the teacher has more than one section of the same subject, she compiles four quizzes for the week, labeling each quiz with a different Roman numeral. Since all quizzes are based on concepts learned prior to this week, students can take any one of the quizzes on any given day. Therefore, the quiz given each day can be rotated among the different sections to deter student copying. The teacher pre-determines the quiz order for each section beforehand.

	M	T	W	TH
period 1	I	II	III	IV
period 3	IV	I	II	III
period 5	III	IV	I	II

The quiz answers for each class section are kept in a separate teacher folder with the corresponding quiz order (above) attached to the outside of the folder to minimize confusion.

E. Who Takes the Quiz?

Everyone who is in class! Because of the nature of the quiz content, no student is excused from taking the quiz, even those who have been legally absent during any of the three preceding days. This strategy eliminates any pre-class discussion of whether or not a student can sit out a quiz, and also clearly establishes the daily student expectation early in the semester. The number of quiz questions asked daily is determined at teacher's discretion, but it should be the same number for every day, largely to simplify the recordkeeping process. Also, the quiz is given every school day of the week that class meets, except on the day that the weekly test is given.

There is an extra (bonus) quiz question asked on the last quiz of the week, so that students have an opportunity to add an extra point to their overall score. The bonus question on both the last quiz of the week and the weekly test (as seen in the following pages) is designed to assess the extent to which the student has understood *why* the solution he has chosen actually solves the problem, and enhances student ability to discuss why it works. This allows the teacher to evaluate students' comprehension of the mathematical concept. Significant errors on this bonus question will indicate a need for re-teaching.

F. Recording the Quiz Grade

1. Student's Record

The student records the number of his correct answers on the quiz record sheet in his folder each day. At any time during the week, both he and his parents can review his quiz status.

2. Teacher's Record

Each day, after the teacher has collected and reviewed the quizzes, the number of questions answered correctly by each student is recorded in the official grade book. This provides a double check for the attendance record, and enables the teacher to identify anyone who failed to submit his quiz sheet.

On the last quiz day of the week, the teacher totals the number of correct answers for the week, including the bonus answer if correct, and places that number over the total number of questions asked for the week, excluding the bonus question. The resulting percentage (%) is recorded as the week's quiz grade.

3. Sample Quiz Records:

a. For Student Present All 4 Quiz Days:

	M	T	W	TH	F
Gradebook	4	3	5	90	

The student scored 6 correct of six questions asked on Thursday; the correct bonus answer is included in numerator but the bonus question is not included in the denominator, reflecting 18/20 or 90% for the week.

b. For Student Present 3 Quiz Days (one excused absence)

	M	T	W	TH	F
Gradebook	4	3	5	ex-80	

Student scored 12 correct answers, excluding bonus on Thursday, out of 15 questions attempted, for 12/15 or 80%. Excused absentees are not held responsible to make-up missed quizzes.

c. For Student Present 3 Quiz Days (one unexcused absence)

	M	T	W	TH	F
Gradebook	3	4	0 (un)	65	

Student has 13 correct answers, (0 correct answers are recorded for unexcused absence). Correct bonus answer is included on Thursday, but student is held responsible for quiz given when he was **unexcused;** so the questions asked on that day are included. Therefore, all questions except bonus are included in the denominator; all correct answers are included in numerator for 13/20 or 65%.

G. Quiz Conclusion: Climbing to the Top

In summary, the cumulative quiz component serves several important purposes. It provides a vehicle for reflecting students' daily effort in their overall grade, while serving the important function of keeping students focused on the instructional process. As a classroom management tool, it enables the teacher to begin each class with a minimum of wasted instructional time. Most important, it provides daily reinforcement of prior learned concepts by including questions on those concepts repeatedly.

In the following section, note that the cumulative weekly test has aspects similar to the daily quiz, but primarily only in the sense that most weekly test questions are based on information taught prior to this week.

III. Staying On Top: Cumulative Weekly Tests

A. Introduction

This component should be clearly distinguished from the prior component describing the cumulative daily quiz. The purpose of the daily quiz is to quickly reinforce earlier skills with a brief test of four or five questions. It effectively jump-starts the daily instructional learning process. The weekly cumulative test is longer, and assesses more in-depth understanding of prior learned concepts. (Those opposed to too much testing should consider that the time devoted here to taking this test adds as much to the learning process as the time devoted to instruction. It is the test taking process, not the product, that forces students to recall, analyze and reinforce prior learned concepts.)

In many traditional classrooms, weekly or bi-weekly tests are administered to assess whether students have learned the skills that were taught during the preceding week, or since the administration of the last in-depth test. Unlike the traditional testing model, the tests used with the *CRCS* instructional approach are more cumulative in nature.

B. Reaching Back

With *CRCS*, only ten to twenty percent (10-20%) of the cumulative test questions is based on the most recent material presented. When tests are given weekly, which seems to be the most effective frequency for students whose learning ability has been assessed to be at a lower level, the questions on new material may constitute as little as five percent (5%).

1. Benefits of Testing Approach

It has been shown over several years that this testing approach has many benefits, especially to students.

Since only 5-20% of the questions are based on the current week's work, all students present on test day can be required to take the test. Although these students may not do well on concepts taught in their absence, they will still be able to fare reasonably well on their grade because at least 80% of the concepts were taught before their excused absence. Students with unexcused absences will likely have different consequences.

The inclusion of questions based on all prior semester learning motivates the student to refresh these skills regularly; students are not easily able to compartmentalize earlier concepts and set them aside from consideration until the final exam.

Students are required to retain corrected copies of the most recent two or three weekly tests in their folder pockets which are designed for this purpose. These tests have three benefits:

a. They are used by all students as study guides for the next cumulative test, since the concepts tested earlier will likely be seen in repeat questions.

b. When students are newly enrolled in the class anytime during the semester, these prior tests give an excellent outline of concepts covered prior to their enrollment, which provides a significant edge toward finding their place in class.

c. The prior tests enable parents to remain informed of teacher expectations as they attempt to help their children by supporting their preparation for the next weekly test.

2. Cumulative Testing: The Essence of CRCS Philosophy

The focus on testing cumulative information repeatedly is consistent with the underlying philosophy of *CRCS*. Student learning is retained when it is constantly reinforced. This approach is also based on the premise and the very firm belief that all students can learn. Since some students may require more instructional time to fully understand new concepts, they will likely be quickly confronted with failure if the entire test is based on this week's concepts. Tests designed for use with *CRCS* are not intended to give full focus on one concept. Rather, the intent is to enable students to identify a broad array of concepts repeatedly. Since the final examination for the course is made up of the same broad array of concepts, students are better prepared to succeed on it.

C. Composition of the Cumulative Test

1. Same Concepts; Different Problems

Since most test items are of a cumulative nature, it is important to emphasize that although the concepts tested are repetitive, the actual test items designed to assess understanding of these concepts are not. Every test consists of new problems unseen on prior tests. Reviewing the prior test questions may help the student recall and articulate the concept, but memorizing former test problems will not aid the student on the current test. The concepts will be the same, but the student must be able to apply the concepts to a new set of data. Further, as required by the new national standards, students now will also be expected to explain *why* the application works.

A sample cumulative test consists of thirty four items; as seen before with the daily quiz, the last item is a bonus question designed to assess student overall understanding of the concept taught. The denominator for determining the percentage grade is 33. The numerator, however, will be the total number of correct answers, including the bonus answer. Just as with the daily quizzes, students will receive an opportunity to increase their final grade, so the bonus question is not included in the denominator. Conceivably, in this example, a student with all correct test answers could score 34 /33, or 103%.

2. Reviewing Test Results

Ideally, the teacher returns the corrected tests to the student while they are taking the daily quiz in the first class after the cumulative test was administered. It is strongly recommended that the teacher make the corrected tests available for review at this time, if at all possible. The test is generally given on the last day of the week; the student should receive feedback at the earliest possible time in order for it to be meaningful. Since homework assignments are rarely given over the weekend, the class time generally used for homework review after submission of the quizzes can be used for review of the weekly test.

Because the test is cumulative, the test of prior skills is generally not difficult for students, but errors may occur if more recent concepts are not fully understood. Perhaps surprisingly, at least seventy percent of incorrect test answers are the result of careless errors in the calculation process. It is actually an encouragement to the student when he realizes this as he prepares his test correction sheet. Careless errors are easily overcome with striving for greater accuracy; correction of misunderstood concepts is more difficult.

3. Test Correction Sheet

Students are allowed up to a week to prepare corrections for any missed questions on the weekly test. This correction sheet must be submitted no later than the day before the next weekly test. The teacher then records the correction sheet as an extra credit homework, that is, it can be used to replace any homework assignment that the student has failed to submit. To enhance the student's ability to do the needed corrections, all solutions to the test questions are posted on the bulletin board and on the computer, after the test has been returned, and all test makeups have occurred. Since the student is provided with the *correct answers*, he is required to show on the correction sheet the work that he did to arrive at these answers.

D. Importance of CRCS Bulletin Boards

It is important to emphasize the significance of the CRCS bulletin board to student understanding (see Appendix #3 - Sample Bulletin Boards). The components that comprise the CRCS board form the compass which points to student understanding of the CRCS learning process. It includes everything necessary to keep students aware of the daily expectation.

The primary posting is a clear statement of classroom rules and consequences, the same that is included in each Student Folder. The students are reminded daily of expectations for their behavior. Also, the teacher attaches a manila folder which contains yesterday's class notes and homework assignment, enabling all students to stay current with classwork, despite absences. Once all students have completed the weekly test, the teacher posts the answers to the test so that students can create their test correction sheet. Finally, a sample Student Folder is displayed, so that the class can check it to be certain that theirs is in order.

IV. Conclusion

In this chapter, we have seen how the more mechanical or procedural components come together to form the structure for the *CRCS* teaching model. Now that the framework has been established, other chapters will focus on the teacher's preparation for the substantive instructional components, lesson development, lesson presentation, supervised practice, and on other supplementary issues.

The Fifth Rung: Lesson Planning, Analysis And Design

I. CRCS' Most Important Concept: Planning, Developing and Presenting a Lesson

This chapter emphasizes the importance of avoiding excessive reliance on textbooks, the importance of always being cognizant of the Order of Things, and the importance of seeing the Big Picture. Most importantly, the teacher always keeps the student at the center of the learning environment.

The *CRCS* model makes a distinction among planning, developing and presenting a lesson. All three of these phases require careful consideration by the teacher, but lesson development clearly requires the most teacher time and focus.

A. Planning a Lesson

As teachers know, ***planning a lesson*** generally involves writing down the topics that the teacher plans to teach during a given period of time. The lesson plan usually includes the goal of the lesson, materials needed, etc. It often refers to specific sections of the textbook that will be covered. These plans are turned in to administrators for review, but partially to be certain that there is a lesson guide available to a substitute in the event of teacher absence. All teachers know how to write a lesson plan and the *CRCS* program does not attempt to alter this; rather, the goal here is to reinforce the importance of keeping students at the center of the planning process.

B. Developing a Lesson

Developing a lesson occurs after ***planning*** and before ***presentation***. It involves a very thorough analysis beforehand by the teacher of the new concept to be presented to the student in his next lesson. ***Lesson development is truly the crux of the CRCS instructional strategy.*** It forces the teacher to stop and think carefully through all of the ramifications of the material she will present. The teacher gives serious attention to the *Checklist for Developing a Lesson*, created as part of the *CRCS* approach.

C. Presenting a Lesson

Finally, *Presenting a Lesson* requires teacher forethought in the actual design of how a new concept will be presented, so that students receive maximum benefit. The presentation usually involves a series of steps ranging from describing the new concept, to conducting a discussion of its application, to solving sample problems.

Each of these three phases is essential to creating a successful learning environment for students.

II. Planning A Lesson

Although *CRCS* does not alter the way in which teachers make lesson plans, the model does recommend attention to the *order in which a topic is presented* and to the materials that are used. These choices must be made through the central focus on the students' learning styles and needs.

A. The Order of Things

Don't let the textbook rule the time at which you teach a particular skill. If the next section in the text is dependent on the skill you taught today, then don't teach that section next. The student has not yet had enough reinforcement time to have mastered today's skill. This is a major flaw in many textbooks, which *CRCS* addresses by allowing enough skill development time through repetition to enable the student to feel confident to build on it. To allow this, the teacher should first go on to another topic that is required, but not dependent on this skill; students can practice and master the skill simultaneously with new material. This is a great benefit of *CRCS*: skills are cumulatively and continuously reinforced from the first day of class until the last, but they are not presented as the required foundation for a new concept until they have been thoroughly mastered. When students have reached mastery, the new dependent concept can be presented.

For example, textbooks traditionally present Least Common Multiple (LCM) just before presenting Adding and Subtracting Fractions with unlike denominators. This sequence, however, gives students only one or two days to master LCM, a skill that is essential to the next lesson. In a cumulative setup, there is clear advantage to teaching LCM several lessons before Adding and Subtracting Fractions. Doing so provides time for the skill to be reinforced and repeated almost daily and ensures mastery of a skill essential to the next related topic, i.e., Addition and Subtraction of Fractions. In the interim, the class will go forward to another topic not dependent on mastery of finding the LCM. To accomplish this, however, the teacher will need to exercise judgment about the best flow of learning, rather than automatically accepting the order in which concepts are presented in the text.

B. Other Examples of Dependent Skills:

1. Leave a space of time between teaching Addition of Integers and teaching Subtraction of Integers. Subtraction is too dependent on addition to be taught the day after addition is taught. Students need additional reinforcement time in order to master the addition concept before moving on to subtraction.

2. Simplifying Algebraic Fractions should be mastered well before beginning other fraction operations. All other fraction operations depend on students' ability to simplify, so that skill requires mastery before moving on.

3. Division of Whole Numbers depends on the mastery of Multiplying Whole Numbers, so a sufficient space of time should be left between these two concepts so that multiplying can be fully mastered.

Allowing students time to master these skills only means that we should teach another topic unrelated to these skills in the interim. This is the beauty of teaching cumulatively. The students may be practicing multiplication every day on the quiz and weekly on the test while learning an entirely new, perhaps unrelated, concept prior to beginning division.

C. Seeing the Big Picture

Many teachers have become so dependent on the sequence of topics presented in the textbook that they sometimes fail to see *The Big Picture: the child's total learning experience*. It is understandable that teachers could lose sight of this, since the demands on teacher time have become overwhelming during the past several years. Nevertheless, it is very important that the teacher maintain a clear vision of student needs. Doing so is essential to the teacher maintaining control of the instructional process.

Peter Airasian describes this in very specific detail in his book, *Classroom Assessment.*

> ...given the variety of instructional demands on all teachers, it is not surprising that so many rely heavily on textbooks and textbook resources to help them decide what will be taught, in what order, and with what intended pupil outcomes. In a real sense, the text publishers have made it possible for the instructional materials they sell to direct teachers in planning, providing, and assessing instruction. However, to use text materials uncritically, and without reference to time and pupil needs is to abdicate one's own assessment and decision making responsibilities. ...But the pupil outcomes, topics, and organization in textbooks do not always take into account the status and needs of every group of pupils, nor do they reflect completely the educational outcomes sought by states and communities.
>
> Although textbooks are undoubtedly the most important resource teachers use when planning and carrying out instruction, this does not mean that textbooks should be relied on exclusively. It is incumbent on all teachers to assess the status and needs of their pupils, the curriculum requirements of their state or community, the sequential demands of the subject matter, and the resources available when planning instruction for their pupils. In the end, the decision about what to emphasize rests with the individual teacher, who knows his or her pupils better than anyone else and who is in the best position to plan and carry out instruction that is suited to their needs.[27]

In other words, the textbook is a guide, not a god!!! Teachers must always stay focused on the immediate learning needs of students, and in following the textbook too closely, they may lose sight of this.

III. Developing a Lesson

Teachers are fully aware of the need for planning and presenting a lesson, but in light of the current demands on educators, we may sometimes find ourselves skimming over the top of the most important of these three phases, *developing the lesson beforehand.* This is clearly a very time-consuming process, which fortunately becomes less demanding as teachers acquire more skill and experience.

A. Six Questions of Lesson Development

Question One: What previous skills are required for mastery of this concept?

As teachers, we need to consider seriously the skills our students need to have mastered prior to being able to understand the new concept. We cannot expect students to change a decimal to a fraction if we are not certain that our students know the place values in decimals and how to read and write decimals. We also need our students to have a good understanding of how decimals and fractions both represent the same thing. In addition, students need to know how to simplify fractions since they are expected to simplify the fraction they find when changing a decimal to a fraction. These skills represent some of the essentials required of students if they are to be successful in making the transition from decimals to fractions. It is critical that teachers anticipate the concepts his students must have already mastered before being able to understand today's lesson. Otherwise, some students will be lost and discouraged very quickly.

Question Two: Of the above skills, which do your students need to review?

Because of the cumulative nature of *CRCS*, the list of skills the students need to review should be short. When using *CRCS*, students will remember quickly how to use a particular skill since they have seen it repeatedly on quizzes and tests. Nonetheless, teachers should take the time to review the skills with their students before going forward with a new topic.

Question Three: How can you relate the skill to something in the real world?

Relating each new topic to the student's everyday world is critical to motivating learning. There are many ways to do this, for example, in changing decimals to fractions. One way is to compare the decimal to cents and then determine what fractional part of a dollar those cents represent. For example, $0.10 (ten cents) is ten out of one hundred cents in a dollar. That is 10/100 or 1/10 (one tenth) of a dollar.

Realistically, not all skills or concepts lend themselves readily to application in the real world, but teachers should demonstrate this application as often as they can, or better, let the students demonstrate applications.

Question Four: How much depth do you expect from today's lesson?

In the decimal to fraction example, teachers need to consider how many decimal places they will be using in the lesson. Only the teacher knows how much his students can learn effectively in one lesson, be that one, two, three, or more decimal places. It is important that the teacher make that judgment ahead of time for his students. Once again, the goal is to have ALL students understand what is going on and the depth of the lesson definitely affects this.

Question Five: What are the steps involved?

Many skills have a list of steps that the students can follow to be successful in arriving at the correct answer. For example, when changing a decimal to a fraction these are some possible steps a teacher might use:

Example: Change 0.25 to a fraction in lowest terms.
Steps

1. Use the numbers in the decimal as the numerator of the fraction.

2. Determine the decimal place value (in this case hundredth's place), and use this as the denominator of the fraction.

3. Simplify the resulting fraction if possible.

Question Six: What homework is appropriate to assign?

The teacher's response to this question should be based on what she actually taught, not on what she thinks she taught, or what she had hoped to teach.

Part of the *CRCS* philosophy is that parents should not be required to help their children practice a skill or concept that was taught by the teacher. If a student does not have the skill to do his homework, there are a few things that might have happened. Among these are: the teacher did not explain the concept or skill properly; the student was not paying attention or did not take proper notes; the homework has more difficult problems than the examples done by the teacher. Often, the teacher is responsible for the student's lack of ability to do the assignment. When a *CRCS* teacher has any doubt that all the students will be able to do the planned assignment, then the assignment should not be given that day. *CRCS* teachers have alternate assignments ready, should this occur. The planned assignment can then be given another day, perhaps the next day, when all students have enough understanding to complete the assignment on their own.

B. Application and Analysis

The following are examples of how to apply the six questions at different grade levels:

EXAMPLE 1: SOLVING SYSTEMS OF EQUATIONS USING THE ADDITION METHOD (SECONDARY LEVEL)

Example: Solve the system: $3x-3y = 6$ and $3x + 3y = 0$

Question One: What previous skills are required for mastery of this skill?

1. Adding polynomials
2. Adding integers
3. Solving equations
4. Evaluating expressions for a specific value of a variable
5. Writing ordered pairs

Question Two: Of the above skills, which do your students need to review?

1. Adding polynomials
2. Evaluating expressions
3. Writing ordered pairs (x,y)

Question Three: How can you relate the skill to something in arithmetic, the students' past, or the real world?

Example: To add polynomials, line up the x terms and the y terms as you would line up the one's place, ten's place, etc. in arithmetic. Therefore, x terms under x terms, y terms under y terms; just like ten's place under ten's place and one's place under one's place. Using the properties of addition also works.

$$\text{Add } 4x + 3y \text{ and } 3x + 2y$$

Line up like terms: $4x + 3y$
$$\underline{3x + 2y}$$
Then add $\quad 7x + 5y$

Question Four: How much depth do you expect from today's lesson?

Use systems that will eliminate one variable using only addition. Save subtraction for a later lesson. Use systems that only involve integers.

Question Five: What are the steps involved?

Example: Solve the system by addition:

$$3x - 3y = 6 \text{ and } 3x + 3y = 0$$

			Steps
1.	$3x - 3y = 6$ $\underline{3x + 3y = 0}$	1.	Line up the like terms: x's under x's, y's under y's
2.	$6x + 0 = 6$	2.	Add the equations together.
3.	$x = 1$	3.	Solve the single variable equation.
4.	$3x + 3y = 0$ $3(1) + 3y = 0$ $3 + 3y = 0$	4.	Substitute the value of $x = 1$ into either of the original equations to find the value of y.
5.	$3y = -3$ $y = -1$	5.	Solve the equation for y.
6.	$(1, -1)$	6.	Write the ordered pair $(1, -1)$. This is the answer.
7.	$3x - 3y = 6$ $3(1) - 3(-1) = 6$ $3 + 3 = 6$ $6 = 6$ $3x + 3y = 0$ $3(1) + 3(-1) = 0$ $0 = 0$	7.	Check the answer in BOTH equations (using substitution principle).

Question Six: What are the appropriate problems to be assigned?

Only those problems that can be solved by addition are appropriate; the topic is addition, not subtraction or other operations. Also, the problems must not include fractions or decimals in either the question or the answer, because the class has not yet practiced these.

EXAMPLE 2: SOLVING PROPORTIONS (MIDDLE SCHOOL LEVEL)

$$\text{Solve the proportion } \frac{4}{x} = \frac{12}{15}$$

Question One: What previous skills are required for mastery of this skill?

1. The meaning of fraction and ratio

2. Simplifying fractions

3. The meaning of proportions and how they are formed

4. The meaning of extremes and means in a proportion

5. In a proportion, the product of the "means" that is, x and 12, is equal to the product of the "extremes", that is, 4 and 15

6. Solving simple equations

   $12x = 60$

   $x = 5$

Question Two: Of the above skills, which do your students need to review?

1 In a proportion, the product of the means is equal to the product of the extremes

2 Solving simple equations

Question Three: How can you relate the skill to something in the students' past, the real world, or to something to arithmetic?

Relate to a recipe. If it takes 3 cups of sugar to make 8 cupcakes, how many cups of sugar are needed to make 12 cupcakes?

Question Four: How much depth do you expect from today's lesson?

Use proportions that have only whole numbers, as these are easier for the students to check. Once the students are comfortable with the steps for solving proportions in general, use proportions with fraction or decimal answers.

Question Five: What are the steps involved?

Example: Solve the proportion $\dfrac{4}{x} = \dfrac{12}{15}$

1. $\dfrac{4}{x} = \dfrac{12}{15}$

$\dfrac{4}{x} = \dfrac{4}{5}$

1. Simplify either side of the proportion if possible.

2. $4x = 20$

2. Cross multiply.

3. $\dfrac{4}{4} = \dfrac{20}{4}$

3. Divide both sides by the coefficient of the variable (4).

4. $x = 5$

4. Solve the resulting equation.

5. $\dfrac{4}{x} = \dfrac{12}{15}$

$\dfrac{4}{5} \times \dfrac{12}{15}$

$60 = 60$

5. Check the proportion using $x = 5$. Always check in the original proportion.

Question Six: What are the appropriate problems to be assigned?

Again, not on what you think you taught, but on what you believe the students learned. The problems are appropriate if they have whole number solutions and all students have mastered the steps.

EXAMPLE 3: DIVISION OF WHOLE NUMBERS (FOURTH GRADE LEVEL)

Question One: What previous skills are required for mastery of this skill?

1. A strong background in multiplication facts.

2. The ability to multiply a several digit number by a one digit number.

3. An understanding that division is repeated subtraction.

Question Two: Of the above skills, which do your students need to review?

They only need to review the concept that division is repeated subtraction.

Question Three: How can you relate the skill to the real world, the students' past or something in arithmetic?

Choose a word problem that requires solution by division.

Question Four: How much depth do you expect from today's lesson?

Use only problems that have zero for a remainder until the students have mastered the steps.

Question Five: What are the steps involved in learning this skill?

Here it might be helpful to use a pneumonic expression to help the students remember the steps. The steps are **Divide, Multiply, Subtract, Compare, Bring Down.** The pneumonic phrase may be as silly as it **Doesn't Make Sense Charlie, But Do** it.

Example: 147 divided by 3

Steps

1.
$$3\overline{)147}$$ with 4 above

1. **D**oesn't

1. **D**ivide

There are 4 three's in 14

2.
$$3\overline{)147}$$ with 4 above, 12 below

2. **M**ake

2. **M**ultiply

4 x 3 and place the result (12) under the 14

3.
$$3\overline{)147}$$ with 4 above, -12, 2 below

3. **S**ense

3. **S**ubtract

14 – 12 = 2

4. 2 is less than 3

4. **C**harlie

4. **C**ompare

The number resulting from the subtraction (2) must be smaller than the divisor, (3) and it is.

5.
$$3\overline{)147}$$ with 4 above, -12, 27 below

5. **B**ut Do It

5. **B**ring Down

Because there is a number to bring down, ALL steps must be repeated.

6.
$$3\overline{)147}$$ with 49 above, -12, 27 below

6. **D**ivide

There are 9 three's in 27

7.
$$3\overline{)147}$$ with 49 above, -12, 27, 27 below

7. **M**ultiply

9 x 3 and place the result (27) under the 27

8.
$$3\overline{)147}$$ with 49 above, -12, 27, -27, 0 below

8. **S**ubtract

27 – 27 = 0

9. 0 is less than 3

9. **C**ompare

0 is less than 3

10. There are no new numbers to bring down.

10. **B**ring Down

It is only when there are no more numbers to bring down that the example ends.

If there is a number to bring down, ALL the steps need to be repeated. It is only when there are no numbers to bring down that a division problem is complete.

Question Six: What are appropriate problems to assign based on what you taught?

Use only problems that have a zero for a remainder until the students have mastered the steps.

IV. Presenting a Lesson

If the lesson has been properly planned and developed, this prior analysis should enhance the clarity of the presentation to the students. The following is based on a fifty minute class period. Since period length may vary, the length of time allotted for presentation should be modified accordingly.

A. Fifty Minute Class Period

In a fifty minute class period, presenting the lesson should require only 18-20 minutes. Generally, this is the length of a student's attention span, so strong effort is made to ensure that every minute of the presentation is productive. After attendance has been recorded, the quiz completed and the homework assignment reviewed, the teacher shifts the tone and attention to today's new work.

B. Steps for Presenting a Lesson

1. *Describe today's new concept*: The teacher provides a brief description of today's concept, using any available visual aid in the room.

2. *Review previous lessons*: Here, the teacher emphasizes any prior concepts learned that will assist in understanding today's new material. It is important here to require students to verbally articulate their understanding of any established concepts that will be needed today.

3. *Prepare class for new material*: A strong motivation for student interest arises from their ability to connect the unknown to the known. As considered in lesson development, here the teacher seeks and provides information that will relate today's material to the students' life experience and/or prior concepts with similar characteristics.

4. *Present new material*: The teacher describes the new concept, encouraging student interaction as much as possible. Help students identify the need for this new information.

5. *Model sample problems*: The teacher puts sample problems (requiring understanding of today's concept) in full view of the students to allow open class discussion of the solutions.

6. *Check for understanding*: The teacher questions students randomly to ensure understanding of the new topic.

7. *Assign appropriate homework problems*: These will be assigned for individual practice. At the teacher's discretion, problems for the individual supervised practice period may be the actual homework problems, to ensure students' ability to work the problems on their own later.

V. Conclusion

It is apparent that the degree of student success is determined by the depth of the teacher's prior preparation and the teacher's willingness to stay on task throughout every minute of the instructional period. By modeling this behavior to students, educators convey the importance that they place on the student's time and hopefully stimulate similar behavior in the student.

Powering The Engine Forward:
Practice And Beyond

As we have seen, the *CRCS* class period starts off with a brief quiz and a check of homework. Then, immediately following the presentation of a new skill or idea, the teacher provides sample problems one at a time with the entire class working together to solve each problem. Time is allowed for questions, re-teaching and teacher/student presentation of solutions based on today's new concepts. Under most traditional teaching approaches, once the oral discussion of sample problems is finished, students are given a new set of problems to solve individually at their desks. Sometimes, this set of problems constitutes the homework assignment.

Under the *CRCS* instructional model, this individual practice time is called supervised practice. This is the period during which the teacher is most actively involved directly with students.

In order to succeed with *CRCS,* it is essential for the teacher to understand fully the importance and intricacies of the supervised practice period. This *CRCS* component is called "Practice and Beyond" because it accomplishes far more than just allowing the student to practice today's concept. Rather, it truly goes well beyond practice and provides the forum for the most capable of students to reach their capacity, while ensuring that every student receives enough individual attention to be certain that he develops a clear understanding of the concept.

This in-class practice time is when the teacher truly puts his signature on the classroom experience. The unique instructional style of the teacher should dictate how the practice period for applying and reinforcing the new concept is conducted.

In this chapter, we will find that the supervised practice period may go beyond the first day of a new concept, and may require a second day of class on the same topic. The teacher will use simple differentiated practice strategies on the second day in order to address a wide range of student understanding. Finally, for those classes where a high level of diversity exists, an increasingly common situation today, we discuss a third approach which is easily incorporated into *CRCS*. This involves a much higher degree of diversified instruction within the *CRCS* classroom.

I. Whole Class Supervised Practice

There is no time during supervised practice when the teacher sits quietly at her desk, catching up on paper work. Rather, this is the part of the class period when teachers provide the greatest amount of direct instruction to individual students. Research has shown that students who receive active individual work supervision from their teachers are more successful than students who spend most of their time working through curriculum materials on their own.[28]

The teacher circulates constantly throughout the classroom, checking each student's progress and providing tutoring as needed. Some students will complete the problems quickly and correctly; they will receive the teacher's immediate positive reinforcement, and likely be given a set of more challenging problems. The teacher continues answering questions and checking on the individual progress of other students throughout the ten to fifteen minute period of practice.

Teachers have been using the whole class supervised practice for decades. In this situation, the teacher has assigned the same practice problems to all students. Even in a *CRCS* classroom, this type of practice is usually effective the first time a concept or skill is introduced. If many students demonstrate a quick understanding in this first day of practice, however, the *CRCS* program strongly recommends the use of a variety of challenging activities during practice time to allow for maximum benefit to all students. By planning carefully, the teacher will be able to incorporate some of the following simple methods of diversification even in the first day of teaching a new concept.

II. Simplified Diversified Practice

Alternatively, there will be times when the teacher determines that the complexity of a new concept has caused most students to miss an understanding of today's lesson, and she may decide that a second day of supervised practice is needed. If there is need for a second day of presenting the same topic, the teacher will want to be prepared beforehand to provide a greater variety of activities, perhaps starting the class off in small groups.

It is important to note here that the normal *CRCS* procedures will still be followed the second day. There will be a quiz on prior material, class notes to be put in the folder, and a homework assignment for the following day. Yesterday's lesson may be presented again, or some aspect of that lesson, which the teacher felt many students missed. The basic structure of the *CRCS* instructional format doesn't change, even when there is a change in the usual pace of presenting a new concept.

The *CRCS* approach encourages the teacher to incorporate varied reinforcement strategies during this practice period. The entire class is still involved in the practice, but this may be done on an individual basis, as described above, or by dividing the class into smaller groups to allow for cooperative learning. Group members may corroborate on problem solutions, but the teacher still actively monitors the progress of each separate group.

This time period enables the teacher to provide for individual differences in student ability levels. Teachers recognize that even though a particular class may be labeled regular or advanced, there are still significant differences in learning abilities and learning styles in every classroom. The teacher has the opportunity during this time period to have some students practice the new concept and to have other, perhaps more advanced, students go beyond that concept and find creative applications. This differentiated instruction is essential to keeping all students interested and challenged. The following examples show some simple ways of adding diversity to the practice period.

A. Worksheets

Textbooks often provide worksheets to enable teachers to diversify the practice experience. These worksheets are usually designed for the varying ability levels within the same class. Also, the teacher often creates his own worksheets. These might be designed beforehand, for example, during the teacher's *lesson development* period, when the worksheets can be customized to the focused topic with problems geared to the ability level of his students.

1. When worksheets are used to add diversified instruction to the practice period, the teacher may quickly divide the class into smaller homogeneous groups and then distribute *different* worksheets based on the level of each group. Students first attempt the worksheets individually, but are then encouraged to work together to complete and discuss solutions within the group.

2. It may be preferable to choose groups at random so that each group is made up of different ability levels. This approach would be based on all students using the *same* worksheet. Then, within these mixed groups, students will discuss possible solutions, giving struggling students the benefit of a broader range of discussion.

Either approach with worksheets allows the teacher to have more time to spend with individual students within each group.

B. Grouping

Grouping is another way for teachers to provide diversified instruction.

1. In a homogeneous ability grouping, the group will be provided with puzzles, games and manipulatives suited to the ability level of the group. This allows students to reinforce the current topic at their own learning pace and style.

2. Heterogeneous grouping may also be used to allow the more advanced level students to interact in a productive manner with students who need more help. This also gives the more advanced students an opportunity to demonstrate their ability to verbalize their understanding of the skill as required by most state adopted mathematics standards. In order for a student to verbalize his understanding of a concept, he must have a very strong grasp of the topic.

3. Another approach to grouping is through the use of computers. There are literally hundreds of programs designed to help students learn mathematics at their own pace and according to their own abilities and learning styles.

In general, grouping allows teachers to use their own creative abilities in helping students to reach their full potential. Under *CRCS*, it is effective for use as the teacher identifies issues unique to each class that could require that students be reorganized in a group forum. It is not, however, the primary source of instruction. Rather, it is used under *CRCS* as one more tool to reinforce and ensure student understanding of a concept, exclusively as part of the practice period; not as the avenue for direct instruction.

III. Highly Differentiated Instruction

A. Purpose and Need

Educational jargon is splattered with hundreds of acronyms, and with terminology that may identify the same thing with several different labels. For example, when a teacher decides to break up a class into several smaller groups, these may be called groups, as we've defined above. Other educators might call these groups learning centers, clusters, team tables and a plethora of different names for the same thing, or often for other things that really don't have the same meaning. Consequently we have an overabundance of terms that may or may not refer to the same idea. This becomes a major obstacle to educators' communicating effectively with both their peers and their students.

Given this, it is necessary for us to establish common definitions of certain terms for our purposes in understanding *CRCS*. Grouping, as considered above, is an informal combination of different students in the same class, used primarily during the practice period for reinforcing concepts. Differentiated Instruction (DI), for purposes of our consideration here, is a very broad framework for instruction that offers multiple approaches to meeting learners' needs. Instruction is presented in many different approaches, with students working in groups or centers almost every day. Direct instruction still occurs always to the class as a whole. There are several specific situations that make this format very effective, and the *CRCS* structure and philosophy can be incorporated into this framework quite successfully.

Before the close of the twentieth century, during the movement to integrate public schools, educators focused on the problems of students from differing racial backgrounds. This was certainly a challenge to teachers of that time, when both teachers and students worked very hard to overcome their fear of the unknown, mixing cultures and races which had barely been known to each other before then. The challenge facing today's teachers is much more difficult to overcome, and differentiated instruction has offered an effective tool in meeting that challenge.

Our teaching practices today must be shaped by an awareness of the extraordinary cultural, linguistic, familial and economic differences among our students. Today, teachers and students face *differing religious beliefs*, with the growth in numbers of Islamic students; *wide ranges in socio-economic levels*, springing from the growing re-distribution of wealth and the fading middle class; and *diverse cultures* which now include a profusion of Hispanic, Asian, Indian and African backgrounds, among others. Twenty or thirty years ago, when teachers were working to receive certification in English As a Second Language (ESOL), we all understood that this was designed primarily to address the needs of Hispanic children being absorbed into the American way of life. Now, teachers try to address the needs of children who speak any one of several different native languages. Our schools in many urban areas are now truly international centers. For these reasons, the implementation of Differentiated Instruction is increasing.

B. Structure of Differentiated Instruction

It is guided by the constructivist or student-centered approach to learning. Like *CRCS*, DI is based on the theory that students develop their learning by building on their previous knowledge. Strong focus is directed toward the student's unique learning style, which in turn generally flows from the student's cultural and linguistic background.

The DI classroom is most often divided into a variety of centers, each one designed to address the unique learning styles of the overall class. In the usual *CRCS* classroom, group work is an intermittent occurrence based on the need for reinforcement of certain concepts. When *CRCS* is used as the instructional strategy for the DI classroom, direct instruction of a new concept still occurs to all students at the same time, even though students may be seated within centers. There may be more hands-on emphasis, depending on student needs. All of the *CRCS* tools are used: there is still a student folder, quizzes, homework and cumulative tests.

In future, as students gain better access to technology, we will be better able to incorporate the use of Differentiated Instruction, where instruction may be tailored very narrowly to each child's needs, and a computer program to meet each child's needs designed accordingly. In the current political and economic climate, however, the education funding required to make technology universally accessible to all American students is not likely to be available for some time.

IV. Conclusion

Regardless of the instructional approach used, the teacher must be constantly interacting with students to ensure effective learning. Using the *CRCS* approach, there is rarely a minute of precious instructional time wasted. The teacher continues to be enthusiastic, energetic and engaged throughout the period. The key to providing an effective supervised practice period for students lies in our ability to recognize and accommodate the degree of diversity within each class. The activities of supervised practice will be dictated by the specific needs and learning styles of students.

Tools For Keeping The Train On Track

This section is an effort to address several issues faced by teachers every day, and to show how the implementation of *CRCS* as an instructional strategy assists in resolving these issues.

I. Classroom Management

The *CRCS* philosophy includes the concept that it is incumbent upon all teachers to develop and display good classroom management skills. Without them, very little learning will take place. Following are some very basic suggestions for teachers who are trying to develop or improve these skills. Fortunately, the tight classroom structure used in *CRCS* makes many of these suggestions inherent in the approach.

A. Classroom Management: Enforcing Student Rules

Students need rules for conduct and established expectations for performance. This provides a sense of security for students that arises from the fact that they can feel certain that they understand the teacher's requirements. *CRCS* recognizes this need by placing the list of class rules and expectations as the very first thing a student sees when he opens his folder each morning. Even though some school populations are very transient, every student must have a folder assembled at the outset of his time in this class, so he recognizes not only what the rules are, but the high priority given to those rules by seeing them as the first thing in his folder. The following are simple suggestions to help guide the teacher's enforcement of rules.

1. **Consistency, Consistency, Consistency**. Say only what you mean and mean exactly what you say. It can't be okay to break a rule one day when the teacher is in a good mood, and then not be okay to break it the next day when the teacher is in a

bad mood. It is very damaging to bend the rule for one student and then try to enforce it strictly with another.

2. **Don't Let the Seemingly Small Things Pass.** If you address what some teachers perceive to be minor infractions the first time they occur, and continue to enforce that standard, you will not have to deal with more serious infractions later. The first time you hear any student speak disrespectfully to another, you should immediately prohibit such behavior. For example, the first time you hear a student tell another to "shut up!", you must make it very clear that this behavior is unacceptable. If you continue to reinforce that position daily, then there is less chance that stronger improper language will be used in your classroom.

3. **When Students Misbehave, Always Follow Through with Consequences.** When students misbehave, always follow through with the consequences you've described to them beforehand. There is no option for, "...if you do that one more time..." This is totally unacceptable in the classroom. Teachers who do not enforce their expectations for student behavior immediately will likely have a difficult time managing their classrooms.

B. Classroom Management: Following Rules for Teachers

Students have to know their limits in order to be secure. They *want* a classroom environment in which they can learn, but they also *need* to know that they are in a classroom where they will always be treated fairly if they follow the rules and show respect, not just to the teacher, but to all of their classmates. This standard of student respect is an integral plank in the *CRCS* philosophical structure.

When implementing this instructional strategy, it is very important that the teachers demonstrate the same conduct that they expect from students. If you truly embrace the *CRCS* philosophy, the following behaviors will follow almost automatically.

1. **Always Speak in a Normal or Soft Tone of Voice.** Raising your voice to students only assures them that they have made you angry. (For some students, this is the goal!) Have a consistent strategy that you always use to get the class' attention without shouting. One technique that seems to be effective is raising your hand. The students should be told at the outset that they are to stop talking and raise their hands whenever they see that yours is raised. If you are consistent with this practice, then in a short time you will have the attention of the entire class. This is just one of many strategies that can be used to bring the class to order without shouting.

2. **Never Belittle or Embarrass a Student.** Just as important, never chastise or debate with a student in front of other classmates. This will force him to respond negatively in order to preserve his image in the eyes of his peers. Remember, the goal of *CRCS* is to enhance student self–esteem, not tear it down.

3. **Never Try to Be the Students' Buddy.** Students have enough friends. They need teachers to act as trusted adults on whom they can rely.

4. **Be Fair But Firm.** Students will grow to respect you when they realize that you apply the same set of standards to all students and that you enforce those standards consistently.

II. CRCS: Enhancing Parent Involvement

A. The Role of the Parent

Nothing can substitute for the importance of parent involvement in the success of the student learning process. Parents establish the standards and expectations of their children in the entire educational experience. For this involvement to occur, the teacher has a responsibility to keep parents informed of all student requirements for the classroom. The teacher begins this information journey on the very first day of school. The *CRCS* approach requires that this communication be maintained throughout the grading period.

It is a sad reality in today's American society that not all students have parents at home to monitor and encourage their educational progress. More than half of our students now live with only one or, sometimes, neither of their biological parents. Many live in foster homes or shelters. In the United States, a growing number of students are actually counted among the homeless, a sad commentary on our country's current political failures. Given these realities, some might question the value of efforts designed to enhance school/home communication. Still, if for no other reason than to clarify course expectations and procedures in a formal way for the student himself, we must continue to try to keep every avenue of communication open.

B. Letter to Parent/Guardian

The letter to parents is discussed with all students on the first day of class. The letter outlines the course expectations and procedures. It makes parents aware of the folder, the homework, the grading practices, the daily quiz and the cumulative weekly test.

A hard copy of each parent letter is sent home by way of the student at the end of the first day of class. Where parents have an e-mail address, an extra copy of the letter may be sent electronically. The letter includes a brief form which the parent is asked to sign and return to the teacher to acknowledge that he has thus been informed of the classroom expectations. A sample of this letter is included in the Appendix.

C. Parent Involvement Through the Use of Student Folders

Parents can keep abreast of their child's activities and daily grades by using the information in the Student Folder. They are fully informed of this in the initial Letter to Parents. As discussed earlier, the folder holds the daily notes, quiz grades, copies of earlier tests and the homework assigned each day. Students are required to bring the folder to class each day and to take it home every evening. The Student Folder is an extremely useful tool for parents, especially in homes that lack access to the Internet.

D. Parent Involvement Through the Use of the Internet

The Internet age has provided a number of options for communication between parents and the school.

- When schools have the necessary technology, parents can use the Internet to access their child's current grades, completed or missing assignments, attendance and student schedules.
- Some schools use an online lesson plan site. The site usually has a section that is available to parents/students to view homework and other teacher notes, videos, etc.

- Many teachers also set up a customized website where they can post notes, copies of letters to parents, news, upcoming events and links to relevant or educational websites, etc.

Aside from the website, most school districts now have automated home dialing/messaging and e-mail distribution to keep parents informed. Teachers can use this source to send informative messages to all parents on record for a single class, or to individual parents of every class. It should be noted here, however, that this system disperses calls or emails to the phone number or e-mail address provided to the school by the parent. Unfortunately, students from the very lowest socio-economic level often live with parents who move frequently so it is difficult to keep phone lists current. These same students come from homes that are not likely to have Internet access. Fortunately, the *CRCS* Student Folder helps to bridge this gap in communication.

III. CRCS and Homework

A. Homework has a Purpose

The purpose of the homework assigned is to reinforce the skills that the student has learned in class. Going to school each day is similar in some ways to taking tennis lessons. An excellent tennis teacher can explain the concepts and skills required for tennis; however, if you don't practice tennis on your own after each new lesson, the skills will not be reinforced to the extent that you can truly make them your own. This is why homework assignments on each new concept are critical to the learning process.

It is equally important that the student leave the class each day with a clear understanding of the new concept. It is not the responsibility of the parent to re-teach his child the concepts needed to complete the homework. Rather, we seek home support to ensure that the student can practice these new concepts in a positive environment and to ensure that this practice does, in fact, occur.

B. Homework and Supervised Practice

The *CRCS* approach requires that, following the presentation of new instructional material, the student has an opportunity to practice the new skill under the direct supervision of the teacher. This period of monitored practice allows the student to question the teacher about the new concept and to clarify the application of new skills. Prior to class dismissal, the student is required to record tonight's homework assignment as the last entry in today's class notes.

The teacher always keeps an alternative homework assignment on concepts learned before today. This is to be used as a back-up assignment in case today's supervised practice time reflects a pervasive lack of understanding of the new concept.

The homework assignment is reviewed the next day, following the daily quiz. Student questions are answered and re-teaching occurs at this point if necessary. Since the concepts were reinforced during yesterday's monitored practice period, re-teaching is not often required at this time.

C. Homework...What's it Worth?

Homework assignments are passed forward for collection the following day, immediately after review of the problems assigned. The teacher places a checkmark in the roll book for this date for every assignment received. The student does not receive a score on the correctness of his homework assignment; to give a grade on practice problems would be unfair to the student. The daily completion of homework assignments constitutes ten percent (10%) of the final grade for each grading period. The number of completed assignments received is represented as a percentage of all homework assigned. When students are legally excused from class, they are required to submit the homework for each class missed. Students can easily find the assignment that was given, since it is posted as the last item in that day's class notes, and on the class bulletin board at the end of each day.

D. The Parent's Role in Homework

As noted earlier, there is no expectation that parents help their children with homework assignments. It is enough that parents demonstrate their interest by providing a positive work setting at home, and by reviewing the student's completed assignments. It is part of the *CRCS* philosophy that the teacher must ensure that the concepts taught were understood. The practice period during class should enable the teacher to evaluate student understanding. It may be necessary to modify the assignment if this period indicates that students have an inconsistent knowledge of the material. There are certainly also times when the student has not made the necessary effort during class time; however, this is a subject for teacher communication with the home and the student.

IV. Technology in the Classroom

In some schools, every student has access to his own computer in each academic class, and every teacher has the same. In many schools, students have no access to computers, but each teacher has his own computer, and can establish clear communication with most homes. Unfortunately, there are some schools in which neither the teacher nor the student has computer access. Therefore, no universal instructional strategy can be built upon the required use of computers. For this reason, *CRCS* was developed in a way to avoid dependence on technology for its implementation. Nonetheless, all types of instruction can potentially be improved through the use of technology, and *CRCS* is no exception. The following suggestions help to incorporate technology into the use of *CRCS*.

A. Smart Boards

Smart Boards represent the latest technology in interactive touchscreen presentation models. Most have screens approximately 50" x 50" and mount typically over an existing whiteboard or in front of the classroom presentation arena. Smart Boards are designed with touchscreens, so writing occurs with the touch of a finger. There are also portable models that can be wheeled around, although they are cumbersome; these have a non-collapsible screen wired to a cart containing a computer and projector.

When the Smart Board is combined with the use of a projector, the PC screen, Digital Video Player, or Document Camera, information can be projected on to the Smart Board screen. The PC, when projected, can be manipulated by touching the screen, basically as if writing with fingers. The software program that accompanies the board allows the creation of interactive presentations much more elaborate than a Power Point presentation. Students can manipulate the board remotely with a miniature board called a MOBI, or they can approach the board and use their fingers to create impressions. Presentations can be made in such a way that information can be concealed until something touches the devices concealing that information. For instance, if a teacher designs a presentation that has balloons covering math problems, a student can throw a soft object such as a kush ball, to break the balloon and reveal a math problem.

B. Responder Systems

A responder is a handheld device with a keypad for students to use to input test answers or other information. It can be used for both formal and informal assessments or evaluations. When students use the responder for the daily quiz, they can do everything on paper, including all the record keeping and graphing of grades, and then put just their answers into the responder. Student answers are viewed *only* by the teacher.

The teacher can use the responder intermittently during direct instruction to determine if students are grasping the new concept. This provides the teacher with immediate feedback about both individual and full class understanding of the new idea. The Responder keeps track of student grades and can present reports to or by students in a variety of ways. For schools that can afford to provide the Responder systems, the recordkeeping requirements for *CRCS* are much easier to meet.

C. Document Cameras

Document cameras can be used in a variety of ways to enhance instruction. The camera will project on to the screen any document that you place under it, including worksheets, notes, maps, etc. The result is similar to that of an overhead projector, except that the document camera projects like a video camera with zoom, freeze and other functions similar to a camera. The camera's ability to provide contrast is especially effective for use with visually impaired students.

D. The iPad

If each student in the class has an iPad the possibilities for instruction are limitless. Students can have electronic copies of everything right at their fingertips, including all notes, folders, handouts, tests, quizzes, homework and even textbooks. All class work can be accomplished on the iPad and the teacher can view from his iPad a real time image of a student actually carrying out mathematical operations.

V. Conclusion

In this chapter, we have attempted to raise points that, although certainly not unique to *CRCS*, certainly serve to augment its success. Teachers constantly seek new strategies for classroom management, and many of these are inherent in the *CRCS* program. Also, parents are an essential element in the learning process, and anything that education can do to keep parents involved and informed is invaluable. Many aspects of *CRCS* focus on enhancing this involvement, especially the approach to homework issues. Finally, although the entire *CRCS* strategy can be implemented without the use of technology, it is significantly enhanced in the classrooms that have the benefit of technology.

All Aboard: Pulling Out Of The Station

I. Starting the Engine: Let's Get on Track

A. Suggestions for Starting: Supporting the Spark or Imposing Restrictions?

Every classroom teacher has his own creative style for presenting information to students. There is no intent in this chapter to intrude on the teacher's creativity. The suggestions below are presented here merely as a set of tools to assist in getting started with the *CRCS* process. This is just an attempt to facilitate the initial effort at implementation, to enable teachers to follow up on their *spark* of enthusiasm about starting a new approach, not to impose restrictions or boundaries. These suggestions will enhance the teacher's spark of interest and provide the impetus that will enable him to implement *CRCS* in the classroom.

The ideas outlined here are purposely very simplistic; most suggestions are truly instinctive to experienced teachers. This entire section may even strike the readers as an insult to their intelligence. Nonetheless, as experienced teachers, the authors know that readers are more likely to implement a new approach in their classrooms if all of the basic preparation steps are outlined in a way that enables them to move forward with a minimum of time and effort.

The chapter is built on the assumption that, once the wheels begin to turn on the track, the actual instructional *style of the teacher* will lead, and will dictate, how the engine is powered; how *CRCS* is implemented. The overall *unique makeup and focus of the students* will dominate the learning environment, and *student need* will drive the process, just as the caboose pushes the train along the track.

Nonetheless, the outline below may provide that bit of extra support for teachers who are willing to try something new, but who lack the necessary time to draft forms and address details which are needed to facilitate the implementation of a new approach. Despite the increase in the availability of classroom technology aimed at lightening the teacher daily load, there is little question that the avalanche of paperwork required of teachers today allows very little time for focus on improving actual instructional strategies. For these reasons, the following suggestions are offered to minimize the initial time demands for teachers willing to try this new approach.

Whether you are implementing *CRCS* at the beginning of the year, or phasing it into practice at some point during the school year, very thoughtful preparation by both the teacher and the student is essential to its success. Ideally, the teacher has ample time during pre-school or on in-service days to structure the framework for student learning. Also, on the students' first few days in class, his direct involvement in constructing the basic framework in the form of the folder, etc., is an imperative element in the development of his sense of ownership of the program and of his responsibility for his own learning success.

B. Pre-school: Focus on the Teacher's Role

Most teachers seek ways of minimizing time devoted to the mechanics of instruction, such as the design of forms, worksheets, and score sheets; they also welcome suggestions that will cut down on recordkeeping. The strongest thread that holds *CRCS* together is the recognition of the importance of preparation and planning, as well as recognizing the importance of a steady consistency in application of procedures and rules. The pre-school period provides the best opportunity to focus on these areas.

1. Prepare Student Handouts for the First Day of Class

a. Student Information Record

This student data was formerly kept on index cards so that the teacher would have easy access on a daily basis to parent contact information. It could more conveniently be kept on the computer, if the teacher has the necessary time to enter the data. For those teachers with access to a scanner, parent contact information cards can easily be scanned directly into the computer.

The student data form should be pre-printed beforehand to include at least the following information: student name, address, class period, home and cell phone, parent/guardian name, workplace, phone and e-mail address. The form is completed by the student on the first day. It is included in the Appendix for teacher copying.

b. Parent Letter

It is imperative to establish early contact with parents to seek their support for the student learning experience. The parent letter, discussed at length in an earlier chapter, outlines classroom rules, procedures and expectations. It is included in the Appendix for teachers' ease in copying or printing for distribution.

The purpose of the parent letter is to establish early communication with parents, and to make them aware of your expectations of both them and their child for the duration of the course. It explains the grading procedures and the weight given to each assignment and test, the use of the folder, quiz and weekly tests, and various avenues for communicating with the teacher.

c. Class Rules

These should be duplicated in pre-school to be ready for discussion on the first day of school. The rules will not be permanently distributed to students until the day that folders are put together. The Consequences shown are posted on the bulletin board, but not in the individual folders. This form is available in the Appendix.

d. Quiz Record and Test Grade Record Sheet

This should be prepared and copied during pre-school for use on the day folders are compiled in class. It is available in the Appendix.

e. Quiz Paper Setup

These are half-sheets of paper kept in the folder, and prepared by students in advance, with their names and class period written on top. At the beginning of class, students are able to quickly take out a half sheet and add today's date, to be ready to start the quiz.

2. Prepare Classroom

a. Set Up *CRCS* Bulletin Board

The use of this bulletin board is pivotal to ensuring that students are aware and reminded everyday of all expectations. Among other things, it will display the classroom rules and consequences, today's homework assignment, and daily class notes so that students who miss the lesson will be able to easily catch up with the rest of the class.

b. Prepare Any Other Bulletin Boards

This will depend on the wall space available, but will include any mathematical formulas, terminology or charts as deemed useful by the teacher. It may alternatively be designed with quotes to reinforce positive thinking, or with cartoons that are related to the class.

c. Arrange Classroom Furniture to Reflect Your Teaching Style

3. Prepare Math Related Activities

a. brief lessons in math to be used for review;

b. puzzles that reinforce math; and

c. class-building activities to prepare for cooperative learning.

The activities listed above may or may not be used during the first week of classes, but it is best to be ready with additional activities. The length of the class period may vary from class to class throughout the day, as often happens during the first week of school as dictated by school-wide scheduling demands.

II. Focus on the First Week of School

A. General Concerns

In most schools the first few days can be very confusing because of varying time allotments for each class, school required completion of paperwork and ongoing schedule changes due to transferring students.

Accordingly, it is important for the teacher to be diligent in recording what is accomplished during each class period to ensure that eventually all classes will have received the same important material. Using the puzzles and other activities that were prepared during pre-school activities will help the teacher to accomplish this. On any given day one class period might be much longer than another, and these activities will enhance student involvement.

B. Day One

1. Welcome Students and Introduce Yourself. Be pleasant but professional.

2. Discuss Materials Necessary for your Class.

    If you have not purchased folders and paper for your students, let them know that they need to purchase these as soon as possible because you will be setting them up in the next day or so. Have your students purchase regular ruled paper, not college ruled, to make certain that all class paper will have identical line spacing on quiz forms. This will enable you to line up several papers in a row to check answers. Students will also need to use number two pencils and any other materials you want them to have (rulers, protractors, compasses, etc.).

3. Review and Discuss Class Rules and Consequences

    This is probably the most important thing the teacher will do today, because it is essential that all students understand the rules and consequences. It will be helpful to project the rules for the class to see as a whole. Take time to explain why each rule exists.

    You may want to encourage discussion among students to be certain of their understanding. The same is true with the consequences. For example, exactly what do you mean by a warning? What is the exact meaning of each consequence?

Do not pass out the rules and consequences until the folders are put together on Day Three. The student's list of rules and consequences is ultimately placed as the first entry in the folder.

4. Distribute and Discuss the Parent Letter.

Go over the parent letter with the whole class if time permits, but in any event, it is essential that the letter go home on the first day. This is when the parents are most interested in knowing what to expect from the class and the teacher. Have the students return the detachable part where the parent signs to acknowledge receipt of the letter. The teacher may want to offer an extra-credit homework assignment to those who return this form timely with the parent's signature.

5. Distribute the Student Information Sheet.

Direct students, step by step, how to fill out this sheet, beginning with the fact that they should not use cursive writing. This information is invaluable to the teacher for use throughout the school year. The teacher should collect these and prepare a binder or record/scan the information to save on his computer. Schools with better technology may already have this information readily available to teachers.

C. Day Two

1. Collect the Parent Signature Form.

This form has been detached from the Parent Letter with parents' signature acknowledging their receipt of the letter. Remind students about the extra homework credit for returning these.

2. Review Class Rules and Consequences.

Continue the prior day's discussion of the class rules. However, again, don't distribute the rule sheet until assembling folders.

3. Remind Students About Folders and Paper.

    Remind students to purchase folders and paper because you will be assembling folders as a class project the next day. Also give some positive reinforcement to those who have already purchased them. Continue with activities prepared in pre-school.

D. Day Three

1. Review Class Rule and Expectations

2. Collect Parent Signature Sheets

3. Assemble Folders as a Full Class Project

    If you have not previously done so, put the folders together. Take time to explain that the folder counts for ten percent of the student grade. Pass out the Class Rules and Consequences, as this is the first page of the folder. The last page is the Quiz and Test Record Sheet, and the second last is the Quiz Answer Sheet.

    Also have the students put loose leaf paper in the back pocket of the folder and some half-sheets in the front pocket.

4. Head Quiz Paper

    Show students how to head their quiz papers. Have everyone prepare at least one. Inform students that quizzes will begin on the first day of the second week.

III. Conclusion: Starting the Engine

This chapter represents an effort to facilitate the implementation of the instructional strategy, *Cumulative Reinforcement of Concepts and Skills* (*CRCS*).

There are many supplemental materials available that might enhance success in the use of this approach, but following the concepts described above will provide enough direction to achieve success. Keeping an accurate record of students' former and final test scores will provide an easy measure of the extent to which the approach has succeeded, and may also enable you to identify aspects of this approach that are more or less effective for your classroom.

Let's get the engine started!

Appendix

1. Sample Parent Letter

(School heading)

    Date
    Dear parent/guardian:

      Welcome to an exciting new school year. Your child is scheduled in my mathematics class, and I would like to take this opportunity to share with you the classroom expectations.

      A summary of the course structure is included here for your review. Most important, you should note that your child will be required to maintain a folder, which will contain everything he/she needs for class, and which must be carried to class each day and to home each night. This enables you to review each day's work.

      Please complete and return the form below so that I can be certain that you have received this information. Don't hesitate to contact me by phone at school or by e-mail at any time if you have questions regarding your child's progress.

      I look forward to a great year.

Sincerely,
Math Teacher

Attachment

Date _____

Student's Name_____

Parent's signature

_____

STRUCTURE AND EXPECTATIONS FOR MATH CLASS

Every student is required to have a folder with both pockets and clips. The folder should hold loose leaf paper clipped in for daily note taking. More blank paper should be stored in the pockets for use with daily class activities.

The homework assignment for each day is recorded at the end of that day's notes, in case parents want to review it. The completed assignment should be placed in the pocket of the folder for easy access. Assignments are not collected until the following day, so that your child should be able to show you his completed assignment each evening. Homework assignments are given Monday through Thursday, and student completion of the assignment will be recorded each day.

On those same days, Monday through Thursday, students take cumulative quizzes based on all prior learned material. This is only a five question quiz, but it is graded and recorded each day.

Generally, on the last day of each week, students are given a more in-depth test, again based on all skills and concepts taught since the beginning of the term. Weekly tests are graded, recorded and, hopefully, returned to students for discussion at the class meeting following the test. After discussion of the test answers, students must prepare a test correction sheet demonstrating correct calculations of all missed problems, to be submitted prior to the next test day; every correction sheet submitted is recorded as an extra-credit homework. Significant learning occurs when students correct prior mistakes. Also, students realize quickly that a high percentage of their wrong answers are a result of careless errors rather than their failure to comprehend concepts. This realization helps them gain confidence.

Please note that all quizzes and tests are cumulative to the beginning of the term, but no quiz will include questions on yesterday's work, and only 20% of each test will be based on work covered this week. The student's final grade is weighted as follows:

40% tests, 40% daily quizzes, 10% homework and 10% folder.

2. Student Data Card

Student's Name_____ Period_____

Address_____

Home Phone _____ Cell_____

Parent (Guardian) Name_____ Workplace_____

Parent e-mail address_____Work Phone_____

Student's Name_____ Period_____

Address_____

Home Phone _____ Cell_____

Parent (Guardian) Name_____ Workplace_____

Parent e-mail address_____Work Phone_____

3. Sample Bulletin Boards

Keys To Success

CLASS RULES	POSITIVE CONSEQUENCES	NEGATIVE CONSEQUENCES
Enter the room quietly and be in your seat before the tardy bell rings.	Success	Warning
Respect your classmates and teacher.	Orderly Classroom	Time Out
Raise your hand and wait to be recognized before you speak.	Learning Takes Place	Parent Call
Remain in your seat unless you have permission to do otherwise.	Learning is Continual	*Referral to Administrator

*Note: immediate removal of any student whose behavior is totally unacceptable

ANSWERS TO CURRENT TEST	FOLDER FOR YESTERDAY'S NOTES DATE/HOMEWORK	SAMPLE OF STUDENT FOLDER
1.		
2.		
3.		
4.		
...		

4. Daily Quiz and Weekly Test Record

WEEK OF_____ WEEK OF_____ WEEK OF_____

Mon_____	Mon_____	Mon___
Tues_____	Tues_____	Tues___
Wed_____	Wed_____	Wed___
Quiz Avg._____	Quiz Avg._____	Quiz Avg._____
Test Grade_____	Test Grade_____	Test Grade___

WEEK OF_____ WEEK OF_____ WEEK OF_____

Mon_____	Mon_____	Mon___
Tues_____	Tues_____	Tues___
Wed_____	Wed_____	Wed___
Quiz Avg._____	Quiz Avg._____	Quiz Avg._____
Test Grade_____	Test Grade_____	Test Grade___

WEEK OF_____ WEEK OF_____ WEEK OF_____

Mon_____	Mon_____	Mon___
Tues_____	Tues_____	Tues___
Wed_____	Wed_____	Wed___
Quiz Avg._____	Quiz Avg._____	Quiz Avg._____
Test Grade_____	Test Grade_____	Test Grade___

5. Class Rules

- Enter the room quietly, and be in your seat before the tardy bell rings.
- Respect your classmates and teacher.
- Raise your hand, and wait to be recognized before you speak.
- Remain in your seat unless you have permission to do otherwise.

Note: Immediate removal of any student whose behavior is totally unacceptable.

6. Quiz Paper Setup

Note: Folder requirements indicate this form is printed on a half-sheet of paper, vertically.

Name _____
Period _____
Date _____

Quiz Answers

1. _____
2. _____
3. _____
4. _____
5. _____

CALCULATION FOR QUIZ ANSWERS BELOW

Endnotes

1   Thomas Jefferson, letter to Littleton Waller Tazewell, 1805

2   Diane Ravitch, *The Death and Life of the Great American School System: How Testing and Choice are Undermining Education*, (c. 2010 by Basic Books), p. 232

3   Ravitch, (p. 200)

4   National Commission on Excellence in Education, *A Nation at Risk: An Imperative for Educational Reform*, (Washington, DC, US Government Printing Office, 1983)

5   Ravitch, (p. 25)

6   Phillip Elliott, *Three Decades Later, Is U.S. Still 'A Nation at Risk'?*, Associated Press, April 28, 2013

7   Michael Petrilli, *The Race to the Top: The Carrot That Feels Like a Stick*, (Flypaper Blog, July 23, 2009) www.edexcellence.net

8   Wendy Kopp, *A Chance to Make History, What Works and What Doesn't Work*, (Public Affairs, the Books Group 2009 (p. 118)

9   Ravitch, (p. 140)

10 Education Week, "Spotlight: No Child Left Behind", pub. Aug 4, 2004, updated Sept. 19, 2011

11 Rothstein, Richard, "A Nation at Risk Twenty Five Years Later" (Cato Unbound, April 7, 2008)

12 Ravitch, (p. 111)

13 Angela Barlow, (Middle TN State University, Murfreesboro, TN) and Huk-Yuen Law, (Chinese University of Hong Kong*)*, *Chinese and U.S. Teachers: Knowledge for Facilitating Disagreements*, (Research Presentation, NCTM Conf. 2013)

14 Andrew C. Porter and Jere Brophy, *Synthesis of Research on Good Teaching: Insights from the Work of the Institute for Research on Teaching*, (Educational Leadership, May, 1988, pp. 74-85)

15 USDOE, *Common Core State Standards for Mathematics*, (Washington, DC, Office of Communications and Outreach, 2010)

16 *History-Social Science Framework for California Public Schools, Kindergarten through Grade Twelve*, (Sacramento, California, State Department of Education, 1988)

17 Ravitch, (p. 232)

18 USDOE, *Built for Teachers: How the Blueprint for Reform Empowers Educators*, (Washington, DC, Office of Communications and Outreach, 2010)

19 Brady, Marion, *Eight Problems with Common Core Standards* (Washington, DC, Washington Post Blog, 2012)

20 Brady, (p. 4)

21 Hung-Hsi Wu, *Phoenix Rising: Bringing the Common Core State Mathematics Standards to Life*, (American Educator, Fall, 2011)

22 National Mathematics Advisory Panel, *Chapter 3:Report of the Task Group on Conceptual Knowledge and Skills*, (Washington, DC, USDOE, 2008)

23 Hung-Hsi Wu, (p. 4)

24 USDOE, *Common Core State Standards for Mathematics*, (Washington, DC, Office of Communications and Outreach, 2010)

25 Frederic H. Jones, Ph.D *Tools for Teaching* 2nd ed. Fred R. Jones and Assoc., 2007

26 Peter W Airasian, *Classroom Assessment*, (McGraw-Hill Humanities/ Social Sciences, 2004)

27 Andrew C. Porter and Jere Brophy, *Synthesis of Research on Good Teaching: Insights from the Work of the Institute for Research on Teaching*, (p. 81)

CPSIA information can be obtained
at www.ICGtesting.com
Printed in the USA
FFOW04n0838150816
26751FF